CHRISTMEN
Experience of Priesthood Today

CHRISTMEN
Experience of Priesthood Today

Gerard McGinnity

FOUR COURTS PRESS

The typesetting of this book was
keyboarded by Gilbert Gough Typesetting and
produced by Computer Graphics Ltd, Dublin.

Published by Four Court Press Ltd,
Kill Lane, Blackrock, Co. Dublin, Ireland.

Gerard McGinnity

ISBN 0-906127-94-7 pb
ISBN 0-906127-99-8 hb

BRITISH LIBRARY CATALOGUING IN PUBLICATION DATA

McGinnity, Gerard
    Christmen.
    1. Clergy   2. Christian life
    I. Title
    248.8'92   BV660.2

    ISBN 0-906127-99-8
    ISBN 0-906127-94-7 Pbk

ACKNOWLEDGMENT

The author and publishers gratefully acknowledge
permission given by Monsignor John Magee
to reproduce the illustrations used in this
book, which were previously published in
liturgical texts issued by the Office of
Pontifical Ceremonies, Vatican City.

Contents

Foreword

Dr McGinnity's new book *Christmen* provides an excellent model for any priest or religious engaged in the day-to-day work of the ministry and anxious to deepen his spiritual life in the turbulent world of today.

It furnishes a clear and much needed guide to the spiritual literature which is available but which by its very vastness and variety bewilders the busy priest. There is much that is new and admirable in this guide and even when treating of what we may call the standard problems of the priestly life Dr McGinnity informs them with a lightness of touch that is one of the special charms of his writing. Moreover, he has a keen eye for relevance and writes for the priest of the 1980s in these islands where life has changed so much during the past twenty years. His experience in giving retreats to priests, his years of training seminarians in Maynooth College for the priesthood, as well as his many holiday periods spent working in parishes both at home and abroad, have sharpened his awareness of what today's priest needs to deepen his relationship with God in a world that is light years away from that of Canon Sheehan or even Dom Eugene Boylan.

How timely his warning that regular retreats (and confession!) are necessary if we are to evaluate our priestly mission, for when we follow our Lord to the top of the mountain only then can we see what we are groping at in the misty valley below.

Even on the supposed contradiction between prayer and pastoral work, this little book yields many gems. It takes the positive line that prayer and pastoral work are of one piece and reminds us too that our pastoral work is not a one-way process, for a priest who is sensitive can be deeply enriched by the faith of those he helps.

The need for comradeship in the priesthood, so evident in the growth of fraternities and support groups, is highlighted. So also is the problem of accepting our loneliness which Dr McGinnity, following St Augustine, places in the context of the human condition and the restlessness that only God can satisfy. It is in this context that celibacy can be seen in its proper prespective.

Finally, there is a most useful chapter on 'The price of caring,' which I would recommend to all priests who so generously commit themselves to the care of others. Recent studies have shown how vulnerable they are to 'burn-out.' Caring is so necessary and so easy, but over-involvement has its perils, to which Dr McGinnity draws attention.

This book is full of warmth and encouragement for all priests and Dr McGinnity illustrates every few pages from his own experience or from a wide variety of authors — poet and philosopher as well as theologian. This tapping of the rich experience of mankind gives the book a depth and a breadth of vision that enhances its attractiveness. The old Irish prayer sums it up well in one phrase:

Dé bheatha-sa chugainn, a shagairt,
A theachtaire Dé ar an talamh.

+ Tomás O Fiaich,
Cardinal Archbishop of Armagh

Priestly comradeship

Two forms of pain which strike priests are boredom and pressure. Boredom arises easily in a quiet rural assignment; pressure, in a hectic urban setting. Georges Bernanos expressed the malaise of boredom in his classic work, *Diary of a Country Priest*.

My parish is bored stiff; no other word for it. Like so many others! We can see them being eaten up by boredom, and we can't do anything about it. Some day perhaps we shall catch it ourselves — become aware of the cancerous growth within us. You can keep going a long time with that in you . . . . It is like dust. You go about and never notice, you breathe it in, you eat and drink it. It is sifted so fine, it doesn't even grit on your teeth. But stand still for an instant and there it is, coating your face and hands.

Boredom is always a potential affliction for the priest. However, in the few decades since Bernanos wrote his striking novel boredom has become a less menacing threat. The more engaging pastoral style prevalent today together with the generally · accelerated pace of life have broken its impact. But if they have, they render us targets to pressure instead.

This opposite sensation of being drained and overwrought is captured in its extreme stages in a more recent literary work, *The Edge of Sadness* by Edwin O'Connor.

They won't quit. Every day I get up, I walk across to the church, I say Mass — and that's the end of the day for me. Because then they begin to come in. Good God in heaven, how can people talk so much? It's endless. My day is spent in listening to one continuous supplicating whine. I know everything they are going to say before they open their mouths: over and over again, the same troubles I've heard for thirty years, the same complaints, the same banalities, the same gossip, the same trivialities, and if you're foolish enough to respond, to actually offer the advice they claim they need so badly, they almost go crazy with impatience. Because you've interrupted them; they haven't finished complaining; 'Yes, yes, Father, that's true, that's very true, but there is one thing more, there's one thing more I've got to tell you . . .'. There's always one thing more. Every day. The same old whimpers and whispers and groans and tears from people who can't manage their own lives and who can't wait to bolt down their breakfast before rushing up to the rectory to tell me they can't.

And it's all nonsense; it means nothing. I'm a priest, not a wastebasket. These people who every morning sing to themselves 'pack up your troubles in your old kit bag and take them to Father' — I want them for once, just once, to stay at home. Or at least to stop talking. To shut up.

The speaker here is clearly exasperated. He is on the verge of breakdown and is losing tolerance as well as his perspective. It is admittedly a highly dramatic soliloquy but for all its exaggeration it alerts us to the crisis which can be precipitated in a priest's life today by demand and pressure.

In the stresses and strains of his ministry a priest needs not only the support of God in prayer but the solidarity and fraternity of his brother priests. Just because he is ordained does not mean that he is above the need for human friendship, company and encouragement. Like any man he wants to feel accepted; he wants to feel he belongs; he wants to feel appreciated. He is liable at times to feel very lonely, discouraged, empty, dissatisfied. There is no use pretending that he is not, at times, angry, depressed or frustrated. There is a great strain in his life if he cannot share or express these strong emotions. Precisely because he is a priest, he does not feel allowed to express openly to lay people his deeper feelings or reveal his frayed nerves.

Because he is a priest he is always expected to be on the job, to be totally available and to be in good form. A young Irish priest whose ministry took him to California after ordination remarked that the overwhelming problems which he met in city life there each day — disintegration of marriages, break up of homes, drug-addiction among youngsters — called for such psychic investment that he found himself looking forward to the dinner each day which was his only form of priest-meeting and his only real human relief.

I think it's no accident that Christ dispatched the seventy-two disciples two by two. He did not intend that they go alone. When sending them in pairs he added, 'I'm sending you like sheep among wolves.' In other words it will be a tough struggle: lots of opposition, a difficult terrain, swimming against the tide. When a man is under threat what he needs most is support. And so Jesus was preparing his disciples for the threatening situations ahead by encouraging them not to try going it alone but rather to recognise the need and value of mutual support in their ministry.

Speaking of 'two by two', I remember as a student doing house to house visitation in Manchester for the purpose of compiling a parish census. We were sent out in pairs and were going quietly from door to door when a non-conformist lady resentful of the Church decided to make a scene. She rang the police, let the dogs out on us and then, to compound the insult, ran along the street knocking on her neighbours' doors alerting people against us. In the embarrassing hub-hub that followed I felt foolish but in a very simple way realised the wonderful difference it can make when one knows one is not alone in the face of opposition. Because that is the weakest moment: that is the time we are most vulnerable and most likely to give in. I am thinking too of a priest I know well who had made a statement on some matter. The press took it up and caused a stir. The priest felt exploited. He went into his office the following morning fed-up with himself, finding it hard to pick up pieces, and discovered a parcel on his desk. No letter. No advice about what to do. Just a token — sweets or something — saying: 'I'm with you: I'm on your side.' It was another priest whom he knew and it meant a lot because it came at a down-moment when the man needed solidarity and support.

It is frightening to think how lonely and isolated many priests have become simply because they feel nobody cares. Frank O'Connor has a short story called *An Act of Charity*. In it he tells a tragic story of a young Irish priest's suicide. The matter must be covered up, the determined parist priest decides. Through the coercion of the doctor and the cooperation of the other curate and the undertaker, no one, not even the dead man's family, is the wiser. The surviving curate witnesses and participates in all this and suppresses his own reactions while the subterfuge is accomplished. It is only after the funeral, as he turns back to his work again that he sighs, in the last line of the story, 'What lonely lives we live.'

In taking the normal human steps to reduce stress and availing of modern facilities and psychological insights to cope with it, we should not deny that some stress is inevitable and can even be positively used if combined with a proper spiritual outlook. Stress can, of course, be looked on as part of the cost of discipleship and a priest's disappointments and anxieties can be related to his work for the coming of Christ's kingdom so as to become a sort of spiritual sacrifice involving his entire being. What is important is that we help each other to respond positively to the stress of our lives. Suffering carried without love can breed bitterness and resentment, and eventually enthusiasm atrophies. In the words of the Irish poet,

Too long a sacrifice can make a stone of the heart.

But fraternal support and spiritual direction can encourage a man to accept pain so that it becomes creative and redemptive in his ministry; he can manage to live it through as his share in the self-emptying or *kenosis* of Christ, who made pain, brokenness and hurt the altar of his own offering to the Father.

But it is a sad fact that many individuals are left to 'paddle their own canoe'; to flounder, very often, in turbulent waters while those who notice are paralysed from intervening by a false sense of respect for privacy.

Stress can accumulate in a priest's life today for a variety of reasons, some external and obvious, others psychological and subtle. Due to the present difficulty in finding housekeepers, the number of self-catering priests is greatly on the increase. One sad consequence of this development is that more priests end up being less well cared for than before. When they do not eat right they are inevitably more prone to fatigue and less able to tolerate stress. They are less alert, less happy, more tense and liable to depression.

Living alone without personal care, a priest lacks so many important checks on himself. He can, consequently, become a victim of stress more easily. The so-called phenomenon of burn-out can become a real danger and, with no one to recognise or point out its onset, a priest can be overwhelmed almost imperceptibly. Some recognised causes of burn-out in priests are difficult transitions — especially in middle years when one has to leave one's own house to take up residence in a hospital or school, overloaded with several odd jobs piled on top of a permanent appointment; long hours — not being able to break out of a never-ending routine; insufficient training for particular tasks which demand continuous input; not enough appreciation from superiors and ingratitude from the people we serve; a growing gap between our hopes and our actual accomplishment, and being too busy working to maintain a regular pattern of prayer.

Sadly the victim is often unable to spot the symptoms and here is where our ministry to each other is vital. The physical symptoms can appear — chronic illness and inability to relax — but maybe the priest has no one at that moment to talk to, or he may be afraid to appear complaining. The emotional symptoms can surface — being depressed or bored by the job, feeling irritable, snapping at people, blaming everyone else, losing drive — but at this stage it's too difficult to take any initiative and share; one's impulse is to shut people out and to resent intrusion.

The spiritual symptoms can begin to show — a loss of freshness and creativity, a loss of hope and self-worth, doubts about our effectiveness and the inability to forgive our own shortcomings; but if a man does not have well-formed channels of communication with a priest director or a small group of priest friends, these symptoms will become pressures to hedge him into his lonely situation.

One source of despondency for some priests is the feeling that they are failing to make sufficient impact on people, coupled with the sad realisation that the Church in Ireland is rapidly suffering the ravage of secularisation. Every priest is painfully conscious of the increasing pressures on people towards abandonment of religious practice.

Research carried out even ten years ago uncovered disquieting trends in Church practice which all hard-working priests will readily corroborate from their experience. There is a greater incidence of drift from religious practice among younger people than ever before. Danger signals were revealed, for example, in a survey among students at university conducted in 1976 by Tom Inglis: 17.2% of Catholic students 'rarely or never' receive holy communion; 34.8% rarely or never go to confession. Between 1967 and 1976 there was a decrease of 26.1% in the number who attended confession more than once a year. The survey found responsible observers to be 'struck by the quiet and deep alienation of a good number of students . . . from the Church and from God.' It has been shown also that people living in urban settings are more likely to lose touch with the Church. When we recall that over half of the Irish population is now under twenty-five years of age and when we recognise that a growing proportion of our population will, in future, be living in cities, we must admit to a growing problem of evangelisation right on our doorstep; to a missionary territory at home. So, concern about our effectiveness in the work of converting people to total trust in God is largely justified.

For some priests another source of despondency and even depression is the dwindling numbers in the clerical ranks. They wonder as they contemplate the decline in vocations who will be at hand to take over where they leave off. It is a fact that in the ten-year period 1960-1970 there was a drop of 1,500 in the total number of clerical students. This represents a ten-year drop of 40% in the students for the diocesan priesthood, a drop of 50% for religious orders and 33% in students for missionary societies. In spite of an undulating graph-movement in the intervening period when numbers rose significantly from time to time, particularly in the year following the visit of Pope John Paul II, (1979), we cannot be unduly optimistic over such increases, since the level from which the growth is calculated is considerably lower than that of fifteen years ago. So there is legitimate reason for anxiety about the future under this head as well.

The average age of priests is rising, which means that an increasing number of those who retire or die will not be replaced. This has meant in some places rationalisation of parish boundaries and personnel. The prospect of such necessary changes inevitably disturbs priests. But it is the pastoral challenge of adapting to new ways and searching for new approaches that tends more than anything else to unsettle priests and particularly older priests. People today are not inclined to hide their criticisms. It is commonplace for people to criticise the Church as too 'institutional.' Young people, particularly, expect it to offer a sense of belonging. They are quick to complain if they do not feel involved or are not consulted in the organisation of Church life at parish level. During the National Youth Congress which was organised in 1980 as a follow-up to the Holy Father's Irish visit one consistent reaction voiced by the assembled young people was a feeling of the Church's remoteness from their own experience, and a claim that they were generally expected to remain passive. They want to feel it is their Church and no matter how efficiently a parish is 'run,' they will claim to be untouched by the Church so long as they are not actively involved in its liturgy and parish functions. Such criticisms can undermine the confidence of a well-meaning, 'efficient' man who is trying to do his best to meet the needs of his people but who feels unable to get through to youth.

What also frightens a lot of priests is a sense of personal inadequacy. Many feel left behind in the contemporary rush to broaden the theological image of the priest. Since the Second Vatican Council, Church documents, enriched by many new or recovered scriptural insights, have been at pains to elaborate on the concept prevalent in the Church since the Council of Trent of the Catholic priest as the one who offers sacrifice. Many priests who have not much opportunity to keep abreast of the vast volume of literature issuing from religious publishers today, feel confused by the plethora of tasks, activities and movements in which they are expected to be immersed; they feel worried that their older simpler view of priesthood does not stretch to cover what is demanded of them now.

These numerous elements of stress are driving many secular priests today to recognise the benefits of fraternity. They are discovering that they face so many eroding influences at work on their spirituality that they cannot afford not to pool their resources. They feel they need each other to help them pray and live their priesthood. I have in mind a man who went off the mission for a year and took up a teaching post in England. He returned to his diocese but felt he could not continue as a priest unless a few class fellows were willing to support him at a deep level, a spiritual level, by meeting on a regular basis to pray together and review priestly life. His friends responded to his challenge and a fine fraternity group grew up around his need. Left alone we can very easily divorce our prayer life from daily work. Prayer and association with fellow priests can, in time of frustration, save a man from giving up or yielding to depression because of failure.

While there is no substitute for rugged personal prayer, prayer by oneself needs to be supported by prayer with fellow priests, if not to survive, at least to be enriched and to develop. When priests pray regularly in a small group each one is challenged to deepen his prayer life.

Such group prayer is a good way of ensuring that personal prayer will not go neglected. Priests who have used a fraternity well often remark on how it sustained them in trying times, revigorated them when their energy was sapped and re-aligned their vision when they were lost in day-to-day difficulties. There are five priests in the fraternity I belong to. We meet each month to pray; we read a passage of the New Testament and we share our reflection on it. In sharing we review our lives to analyse how God has been intervening over the past month and how we have responded or failed to respond. This is a beautiful celebration of Christ's presence in our lives. Openness to Christ in the presence of one another develops a bond. Everyone is encouraging to the man in a difficulty, challenging him to develop his particular gifts. It helps all of us to live our priesthood more and more in the light of faith and to recognise how Christ is trying to work through us. And we need this. 'Priests need priests', an old priest I know used to say repeatedly. St Paul in his letter to the Romans (1:11) says:

I am longing to see you; I want to bring you some spritual strength, and that will mean that I shall be strengthened by you, each of us helped by the other's faith.

One of our failures as priests is that we leave our spiritual life too hidden. We keep it from enriching or benefitting our brother priests. We are too shy about talking about God and his working in our lives. In fraternity we can reflect with fellow priests on our experience of Christ and put ourselves to that extent in their hands to hold us faithful to the demands of our call and help us recognise the graces he gives us. It goes without saying

that this kind of exchange is not easy to develop. It is much easier to relate to every priest at the lighter level of 'Hail fellow, well met.' We are naturally reticent about our feelings and thoughts. We do not care to release them like streamers in the wind and vulgarise what is personal and precious to us. But this is not in question. Our responsibility to one another in the faith is something different.

No priest should feel he is battling along alone. We are engaged in the one work, the Lord's work, not any one man's work. Your struggle today was someone else's yesterday and may be mine tomorrow. Why not share it? You will be relieved by sharing but reassured as well. Maybe you are also reassuring someone else who felt, until he heard you, that he was the only one in his particular predicament. For many reasons I find the experience of fraternity valuable. It lightens burdens I might otherwise keep to myself. I realise that other priests are seriously interested in my work; they reassure me in my doubts; they affirm me in my judgments. I genuinely feel they are sharing responsibility with me. I come away relieved. I also get my work in perspective, for I learn of the difficulties of other men's assignments. Again, it is important to hear the expectations which other priests have of me and to be strengthened by the advice and opinion they offer.

All this takes place in what is called the *review of life*. It is simply an attempt to discover the presence of Christ and his expectations of us all in events of our priesthood over the previous month. We try to ask ourselves and each other how we have cooperated with or impeded his intervention in our lives. This forms the habit of seeing everything we do in the light of faith and draws us, if we let it, to a fuller response to God's will. It is not an examination of conscience. It is an effort to look at our pastoral experience and prayer effort and each month to hold them up against the back-drop of our call. We try to face honestly our basic attitudes and personal values in the day-to-day struggle to preserve them.

Not every man is attracted to the same kind of fraternity in the priesthood. Prayer groups for priests can be as varied as their personalities. I know a retreat team for secondary schools in a certain diocese which has turned into a prayer group. It was set up to prepare school retreats and in fulfilling this function the men discovered the side-effect it had: they ended up discussing their own prayer lives as priests and began praying together. I know a presbytery in a big city where the priests recite the liturgy of the hours in the dining-room after lunch and supper. Visiting priests are invited to participate. At the intercessions, parish needs, especially those of the sick, are included. I know that the divine office is made easier for them in this way; they look forward to it; it binds them together and it develops fraternity. I know others who attend a prayer group once a week which is flexible in size and composition and includes lay people and sisters. I know that they are helped by the very fact that some priests pray with them. Part of the reason must be *their* need for support from and solidarity with priests at a time when so many problems, customs and guidelines in spirituality have altered or been undermined.

Rather unfortunately, the diocesan bridge schools and golfing teams of a decade or two ago are dwindling and disappearing and priests visit each other less. As priests drop responsibility for each other, loneliness is bound to increase. When a man withdraws to a certain level he must find it impossible to attempt to break through to anyone when he is desperately lonely.

While the ready-made structure of diocesan deaneries would seem to offer a suitable unit within which priests might meet regularly, smaller groupings are necessary too. A combination of imagination and sensitivity in even one priest is all that is necessary to create some social or recreational outlet for a group in his immediate area. The reasons for meeting do not have to be lofty ones; what is important is (to borrow a phrase from Antoine de St Exupéry's fox in *The Little Prince*) 'to establish ties.' Some may never need such ties of friendship but sadly, it must be admitted, they did not exist for some who might have found them a strong support or even a crucial need.

Whenever priests meet together to pray about their ministry, the 'spin-off' advantage of mutual support and co-responsibility at a deep, spiritual level is a powerful incentive in their work. It can tip the balance in favour of a productive and fulfilled priestly life for many. Cardinal Newman must have had some form of priestly fraternity in mind when he wrote these lovely lines:

They whom God forces to part with their near of kin, for his sake, find brethren in the spirit at their side. They who remain solitary, for his sake, have children in the spirit raised up to them. How should we thank God for this great benefit! He gives, he takes away; blessed be his name. But he takes away to give again, and he withdraws one blessing to restore fourfold. Abraham offered his only son and received him back again at the angel's voice. Isaac 'took Rebekah, and she became his wife, and he loved her; and Isaac was comforted after his mother's death.' Jacob lost Joseph, and found him governor of Egypt. Job lost all his children, yet his end was more blessed than his beginning. We, too, through God's mercy, whether we be young or old, whether we have friends or few, if we be Christ's, shall all along our prilgrimage find those in whom we may live, who will love us and whom we may love, who will aid us and help us forward, and comfort us, and close our eyes. For his love is a secret gift, which, unseen by the world, binds together those in whom it lives, and makes them live and sympathize in one another.

Failure and reconciliation for priests

When we come to review our lives, to look into "the rag-and-bone shop of the heart", we often painfully recognise that we live at two levels. For brief periods we hit the heights of our ideals but more often we pitifully fall short of them. The words of an Irish poet could sum up that dichotomy within us and the resulting pain and frustration which drives us to regret.

> To drift . . .
> with every passion until my soul is a stringed lute
> on which all winds can play . . .
> Is it for this that I have given away mine ancient
> wisdom and
> austere control?
> Me thinks my life is a twice-written scroll,
> scrawled over on some boyish holiday with idle songs
> for pipe
> and virelay,
> which do not mar the secret of the whole.
> Surely there was a time I might have trod the sunlit
> heights,
> and from life's dissonance struck one clear chord to
> reach the
> ears of God:
> Is that time dead?

Oscar Wilde would certainly not have claimed to be a theologian yet, without knowing it, he put his finger with unerring accuracy on the scriptural meaning of sin: missing the mark. The word 'sin' in the Old Testament is based on an archery analogy.

It helps us understand sin properly if we work from this analogy. When the archer draws the bow but the arrow falls short of its target, sin is presented as a state of mind which obsessively misses the point of everything and so falls back indulgently on itself. And so Scripture also describes sin as death, for it is an experience of frustration within its own limitations, full of ideals which it is never free to fulfil because it never arrives: never hits the bull's eye.

Christ's teaching is radical in that it goes to the root of our sinfulness and offers us the target and purpose of all life — union with God, which will unify our fragmented selves. From time to time various obsessions like false gods play the tyrant in our lives in a humpty-dumpty experience of passing enthusiasms. If we could only realise it, these gods we create are our sins and will ultimately break our hearts when they fail. For God has made us for himself and our hearts are restless and frustrated till they rest in him.

The priest, whose ministry is to offer Christ as the source of redemption and reconciliation for his people, must continually shatter the idols that shape and dominate his own daily life. If he is calling people continuously to break sinful habits and surrender more fully to the warmth of God's forgiving love, he himself must be honestly struggling in his own experience to reject the illusory attractions which come between him and God, which lock him in selfishness and prevent him from living in freedom, strength and love as a man of God.

We may be called to the supreme intimacy with God of priesthood and religious life, but 'these treasures', St Paul reminds us, 'we hold in vessels of clay.' We are weak; we fail if left to ourselves and our own devices. Referring to this fact St James says: 'we all make many mistakes,' and St John: 'If we say we have no sin we deceive ourselves and the truth is not in us.' But what is sin? Surely it is not merely a matter of breaking commandments; that is a narrow view of sin which concerns only external acts.

It was all right for the people of the Old Testament, a people of undeveloped spirituality. It has very little to do with Christ's call to perfection.

'From him to whom much is given, much will be expected'

Christ announced. This is the frightening reality. Because of our religious call we are those to whom much has been given in the way of divine intimacy, divine trust. That trust must be guarded and returns made. Remember the talents; a big return was expected of the man who got ten talents — as much again. The man with five pleased and satisfied the Master only with *five* more. What I am coming to is this: what is sin or failure for us might not be counted sin for a layperson. 'From him to whom much is given, *much* will be expected.' Our privileged position close to the Lord, our share in his ministry, is a challenge more than a guarantee. Peter and Judas enjoyed the Lord's favour equally, they both received the Lord's call, yet both failed and betrayed in their own way.

> Servant of God has chance of greater sin
> and sorrow than the man who serves a king
> For those who serve the greater cause may make the
> cause serve
> them
> Still, doing right and striving with political men may
> make the
> cause political, not by what they do but by what they
> are. (T.S. Eliot, *Murder in the Cathedral*)

For the priest or religious, profession and practice are completely identical. It is not as if we have office hours. Christ's lantern burns with the oil of my life. If I am a mediocre priest it is as if the lantern-panes are grubby and tarnished. I am preventing his influence from reaching people.

Each time we go to confession we should measure ourselves against the Gospel and take a look at the embarrassing gap that exists between what we are and what we are called to become. 'Be perfect as your heavenly Father is perfect' is the compelling call of Christ. This is the only commandment that counts for the priest. The others (Thou shalt not . . .) are all presumed to be kept. Christ wants to take us beyond our negative, minimalist view of the commandments to a limitless self-giving and witness of love. To give away our cloak, to walk two miles, to offer the other cheek. That is probably why someone like St Gertrude would go *every* day to confession. She was not scrupulous or neurotic; just sensitive to the demands of her call and alive to failure.

If we think we have nothing to tell, maybe it is just that we are unable to see what we should be telling. Maybe dreadful mediocrity has become second nature to us and our conscience can no longer summon up an honest protest against it. Maybe we have cravenly distorted what we should be to make it fit what we really are. Maybe we have tailored the cloth to fit our own size and that size might not be very big. Maybe there is nothing to tell because the conscience is not even ruffled anymore. Maybe the level of expectation is so low that we have no bother reaching it all the time. Maybe our standards are so adjustable that they can follow us instead of our following them. Maybe we fit neatly into the mould, simply because it is of our own making. A priest's greatest difficulty might well be that he is not convinced of sin. He no longer recognises it. The contemporary 'eclipse of conscience' with its erosion of the sense of sin may have caused a decline in his moral sensitivity.

A young man, Laman Blanchard, who was hoping to make his name and become established in the literary world as a poet, once proudly sent a metrical contribution of several little poems to Charles Dickens in the hope that the latter would publish them in his magazine *Household Words*. The poems dealt with eastern topics and so Blanchard entitled his contribution 'Oriental Pearls at Random Strung.' But Dickens returned them with a covering note:

Dear Mr Blanchard

Too much string,

Yours C. Dickens.

I suppose this is our fear when we look at our lives before God or when we try to anticipate his reaction to us when we meet him face to face: that he would simply remark 'Too much string.' Too much that is useless and not enough pearls. Not enough that is sterling and valuable and precious. Not enough that is unalloyed and pure. Too much padding.

When Jesus promised the Spirit he declared that one of the

Spirit's functions would be to 'convince the world of sin.'
Perhaps we have dulled our consciences against the Spirit's
promptings. The outstanding difference between the reactions
of Peter and Judas, since both denied Christ, was — in so far
as we presume to judge — that Peter broke down and admitted
his fault.

> O happy he whose heart can break and peace and
> pardon win
> How else may man make straight his path
> and cleanse his soul from sin
> How else but through a broken heart
> May Lord Christ enter in?'

With venial sin what matters is perhaps not so much having
mathematical accuracy as to the precise number of times we
failed in a particular area as recognising the outlook behind
them. Faults and imperfections are instructive as symptoms
of deep-rooted inner attitudes of, for example, sloth,
hardness of heart, unlovingness, unreceptiveness to God and
his love. Little things you do may reveal you as a proud person,
or closed, touchy, inflexible, demanding, thoughtless,
uncontrolled, unreliable, inconstant.

So far from being able to say complacently, 'I don't need to
go to confession, I've nothing to tell', we are faced with the
humanly impossible task of being 'perfect, as our heavenly
Father is perfect.' Only the person who is entirely unaware of
his calling could be self-satisfied; he can be self-satisfied only
because he is not sensitive to the demands made on him. He
will discover all of a sudden that he is going nowhere or perhaps
his tragedy is that he does not discover. He can fall into a groove
and the only difference between a groove and a grave is the
depth! Val Doonican's song 'Everybody's running in a mad,
mad world but nobody's going nowhere' could be applied to
the spiritual life. Without the very definite goal of a closer
intimacy with Jesus, a growth in the likeness of Christ, we get
nowhere, make no advance.

I find in the unlikely spot of the Old Testament an apt image
to capture the positive side of confession for the priest in his
prophetic role. In the book of Jeremiah, chapter 17, we read:

'Blessed is he that puts his trust in the Lord, makes the Lord his refuge. Not more favoured is a tree planted by the water's edge, that pushes out its roots to catch the moisture, and defies the summer heat; its green leaves careless of the drought, its fruit unfailing.' Bearing the burdens of the day and the oppressive heat which saps our spiritual energies — the withering cynicism, the scorching apathy, the blistering materialism — we can only keep fresh in our dedication by relying on the healing and strengthening resources of the sacrament of reconciliation.

Indeed it is Jeremiah who, as leader of God's chosen people in the Old Testament, offers a powerful message of hope to the dispirited priest who is overcome by failure and hopelessness. His message of hope comes by another symbol — that of the potter shaping clay. It would be difficult to find a more apt picture of the positive side of the sacrament of reconciliation in a priest's life. Jeremiah found himself faced with a frighteningly difficult mission. He happened to be leading God's people at a particularly awkward and depressing time in their history. Although they had been singled out by God to be a shining light to the nations of the world, they had become defeated and quarrelsome. On the point of giving up, Jeremiah was directed by God to the potter's house, and there he saw that the potter did not discard the warped vessel even when its appearance disappointed him but reshaped it and remade it into something new and attractive. Jeremiah was reassured that God had power to do the same with him and so with the people he served, when they had become broken on the turning wheels of life.

Our reconciliation is more than confession. It is a redesigning; like Jeremiah we must hear God's word of hope: we must believe that he can redesign. Misshapen by sin or grooved by sinful habit, the vessel of our lives does not defeat his power. His image may have become deformed in us. The disfigurement may have settled in the clay, but his image is never too misshapen to be remade. God, the all-powerful potter, can still envisage what the clay might be and his skilled hands can realise his vision. With God our priestly lives are always a possibility, an opportunity, a new creation.

One is reminded of the emotional and moral depths to which

the Whiskey Priest sinks in Graham Greene's novel *The Power and the Glory.* His guilt and moral weakness haunt him. Ill-health drains his energy and he ends up a nervous wreck and practically an alcoholic. As if this paralysis weren't overwhelmingly enough he loses the last remnants of self-respect when, as a result of a sexual lapse, he ends up with an illegitimate child. And still he can preach with powerful conviction of the infinite mercy of Christ. He refuses to succumb to despair. He fights his shortcomings. Through the sheer fact of being robbed of all human dignity, he is forced to rely entirely on the bare essentials of priesthood and the central truth of our salvation through Christ's death and resurrection. This mystery becomes everything for him and he tries to live it out in the brokenness of his own experience.

Perhaps the most powerful illustration of this truth in recent times is the life of an Australian diocesan priest, Con Kehoe, who recently visited Ireland and told his life-story in Dublin. After ordination he seemed to embark on a priesthood of great promise with numerous talents to bring to his work.

Following on nine years post-graduate work at universities in Europe he returned as a professor to a seminary in Sydney. He soon got involved on the political scene in Australia where the Church, fearing an infiltration of the offical Labour movement by Communists, formed its own. After subsequently setting up his own movement and working against great odds, he experienced so much fatique and tension that he suffered a nervous breakdown. He resisted treatment in a St John of God Hospital and, because of the tremendous disturbance he was causing, had to be moved to a State mental hospital, where he was subjected to very tough treatment. He woke up in a padded cell wearing a straightjacket.

When he roared and howled, an orderly threatened to tighten the jacket further and further. He cursed all clerical visitors including his bishop until one day a parish priest fought with him and forced him to admit his illness and accept treatment. When he eventually recovered sufficiently to be discharged from hospital he felt he needed some support to cope with life. There was no structure to help people who had broken down mentally. So he joined Alcoholics Anonymous though he was not alcoholic, and he followed their twelve steps — admitting failure, relying utterly on God's power to heal him and so on. And when he was well enough he founded *Grow*, an organisation of self-help for people who suffer from breakdowns, a sense of failure, mental disorders or maladjustments of any kind. A priest who failed, who sank into the depths of utter depression, desolation and loneliness, forged this powerful movement on the anvil of his own misery and its influence is now world-wide. Thousands of people are now being helped to believe in themselves again through sharing in a supportive group in which there are no labels — all are equal —, in which they come to accept that they are worthwhile in God's sight and that God has an important plan for each of their lives. By experiencing acceptance and developing confidence they manage to control their lives more. And this has all been made possible for them by a priest who accepted his weakness and allowed God to make it a source of strength. No matter how much we are broken we can still be a source of God's healing to others. His power is at its best in weakness.

Spiritual direction

A priest is foolhardy if he thinks he can go it alone in developing spiritual life. There are certain human endeavours a man might perhaps undertake on his own strength, without guidance or supervision. In such a vital matter as aspiring to holiness as Christ's disciple, can one afford to go it alone? It is an accepted axiom of human experience: *Nemo iudex in causa sua*. All the more is this true of the supernatural experience, which is lived in faith and which has few human supports, where there is so much danger of vagueness because one is dealing with intangible realities. A man can be misled about his own state of soul and above all in regard to his progress, if any, to perfection. There is the perpetual danger of subjectivity taking over. The presence of a spiritual director lessens this danger. He, at least, can be objective, can assess, recommend, comment, check. It is immature to hop around from one director to another, for then continuity is lost and if we squarely face such a tendency we may even discover we are running from something within ourselves. A director must have time to 'tune in' to our wavelength, to appreciate our potential and assess our weakness. It is courting disaster to become irregular in our use of the sacrament of reconciliation and this, unfortunately, is an occupational hazard. We administer it so often to others we may feel we are close to it, whereas in reality we are not applying it to ourselves: we are drifting from it. It is risky and wrong to make it random, to leave it till we happen to be in town buying a new pair of shoes! One reason priests give for their under-use of the sacrament of reconciliation is the absence of an up-to-date scheme of self-examination. Here are two possible approaches.

One approach to priestly self-examination would be to apply the call of the Beatitudes to our everyday life.

Blessed are the poor in spirit Are we living a simple life, fighting against the accumulation of unnecessary possessions and the compulsion to acquire? Do we remove the distracting encumbrances which clutter our lives or do we need to need things? Is there a centre of silence in our day? Do we make room for God to govern our day? Do we entrust the yield of the harvest to his power?

Blessed are the meek Are we arrogant and overbearing? Do we defend ourselves by crushing opponents or sweeping them aside? Do we try to respect, appreciate and accept everyone?

Blessed are the peacemakers Do we possess peace within ourselves? Are we integrated in our personalities, clear of complexes and detached from anxieties? Do we work hard to remove barriers and divisions in the parish?

Blessed are those who hunger and thirst for justice
Are we sensitive to injustice? Do we see justice as the practical expression of love?

Blessed are the pure in heart Do we aim at utter sincerity, avoiding compromise and sham? Do we try to keep integrity and identity? Have we the purity of heart which puts God and his demands first? Have we been popularity hunters?

Another and fuller approach to self-examination would be to take as headings the three ministries of the priest as outlined in the Vatican Decree on Priestly Ministry.

1. *On my Ministry of the Word*:
   (a) Am I conscientious about my preaching?
       Do I prepare my sermons diligently?
       Do I apply the message that I preach to my own life?

   (b) Is my own life a witness to the Gospel that I preach?
       What is my witness to:
       (i) the spirit of poverty?
       (ii) the positive ideal of chastity?
       (iii) Christlike obedience?
       (iv) Honesty
            Do I do an honest day's work
       (v) Charity? towards fellow priests?
            — towards my people?

2. *On my Ministry of Shepherding*:
   (a) Am I conscientious in my visitation of my people
       in their homes?
       in their schools?
       Can I honestly say that, like 'the Good Shepherd', 'I
       know mine and mine know me'? Or am I 'a stranger
       to the flock'?
       Do I tend to neglect the special needs of the poor, the
       old, the lonely, the sick, the underprivileged?

   (b) Do I constantly make myself available to my people?
       Or do I tend to put my own convenience before that
       of others?
       Do I make a conscious effort to be 'Christlike' in all
       my dealings with my people?

3. *On my Ministry of Worship and Sanctification*:
   (a) *Mass:* Do I usually make a serious preparation
            for Mass?
            Do I celebrate Mass reverently and
            meaningfully?
            Or could it appear to the congregation that
            I do not really believe in what I am doing?
            Do I really try to make the Mass more
            meaningful for my people?

(b) *Sacraments*: Do I administer the sacraments reverently and meaningfully . . . or just mechanically?

Do I bring Holy Communion to the sick and aged as often as I should?

In the sacrament of Penance, do I always show the love, mercy and understanding of Christ?

Or do I sometimes tend to be harsh or impatient?

When I receive the sacrament of Penance myself, do I make the occasion a real meeting with Christ?

Do I make the most of my administration at baptisms, marriages and funerals?

(c) *Divine Office*: Do I recite the Prayer of the Church regularly?

(d) *Private Prayer*: Do I make adequate place in my life for private personal prayer?

Do I regularly make a visit to the blessed sacrament?

Do I regularly give time to solid spiritual reading?

A suggested Act of Repentance

For turning prayer into a duty, or neglecting it altogether;

For being a talker and not a listener in prayer;

For talking about suffering, but being unwilling to suffer;

Lord, have mercy.

For saying 'This is my body given for you', but failing to give myself to others.

For careless and insensitive celebration of Mass and the sacraments;

Lord, have mercy.

For not allowing or encouraging the laity to play
their full part in the parish;
For complaining about the lack of vocations, without
acknowledging that my own life, and lack of joy
and faith may attract no one to the priesthood;
For my laziness, lethargy and indulgence;
Lord, have mercy.

For my lack of faith, hope and love;
For allowing myself to be taken in by pagan and
worldly values;
For guarding my popularity;
Lord, have mercy.

For my pettiness and parochialism;
For living by rubrics and not by the Holy Spirit;
For my lack of personal discipline;
Lord, have mercy.

For considering myself superior to others;
For my impatience with the ignorant;
For refusing to be the friend of sinners;
Lord, have mercy.

We have been selective in the places we have visited;
we have found it easy to visit some but have
neglected to visit other parishioners who perhaps
had greater need of our presence;
We have sat in presbyteries and expected people to
come to us;
We have spoken in formulas and cliches because we
have not bothered to know the truth;
Lord, have mercy.

We have not used modern means of communication
to further the spread of the Gospel;
We have been afraid of being considered unorthodox,
and have failed to proclaim the light that is within
us;
We have run away from the task of the prophet;
Lord, have mercy.

If we forget that with the bishops we are the least in
the kingdom;
If we hamper the work of the Spirit in others, and
have harried or bullied God's people;
If we take care of the sanctuary, but neglect the living
sanctuary that is another person;
Lord, have mercy.

If our rule in the parish is autocratic and
self-opinionated;
If we have failed to learn from the laity and other
priests;
If we have neglected other Christian communities and
non-Catholics;
Lord, have mercy.

If we have sat in judgement on the faith of our fellow
priests;
If our treatment of fellow-priests, students for the
priesthood and nuns has made them feel of little
worth;
If our presbyteries are not Christian homes, but
hostels for strangers;
Lord, have mercy.

If we fail to love our fellow priests
If we fail to love those entrusted to us;
If we have failed to be humble;
Lord, have mercy.

We have failed to study the scriptures;
Our preaching has been dull, unprepared and lifeless;
We have scolded the people for their ignorance even
when it has been caused by our own sins of
negligence
Lord, have mercy.

We have been interested in practising Catholics, with
no mind for the others;
We have taught people without first learning;
We have counselled many without seeking counsel for
ourselves
Lord, have mercy.

We have misused our power;
If we have obeyed the letter of the law without regard
    to the spirit of the Gospel;
If we have condemned or judged another;
Lord, have mercy.

If we have failed to be honest or to co-operate with
    each other, and with our bishop;
If we have been hypocritical;
If we presume to be greater than our Master;
If we fail to walk with the poorest, anywhere, at any
    time;
Lord, have mercy.

Prayer

Lord Jesus, we are ashamed of our record of failure
We acknowledge our sins with sorrow and ask for forgiveness.
Help us to rely on your strength and your Spirit
As you forgive us, help us become true ministers of your
forgiveness to others.

A priest's prayer today

Many priests today feel they have lost control of the vast output of prayer literature. They are trying to find their bearings in the treatment of new trends. They are looking for guidance in their efforts to evaluate what is happening in spirituality at the present time. The great modern insights into prayer — the new and recent emphases — could be summed up in a single attitude: 'letting go', 'letting God be' or 'being still with God': simply accepting our hunger for God and making the journey *inwards* — to meet him in the depth of the heart.

Glancing at the broad sweep of Church history one could isolate three main patterns in prayer or approaches to God. It goes without saying that this is a conveniently simplified analysis of prayer trends. It is merely intended to highlight predominant emphases, not to exhaust complexities.

The settled period from Trent to Vatican II could be called an obediential phase. There were defined and set patterns for praying. We learned certain formularies and reached God through the recitation of what was often long and unwieldly terminology. But the terminology remained sacrosanct and guaranteed that we worshipped.

The second phase came after Vatican II when we moved into what could be called the relevance phase. Everything you said or practised had to be held up to the scrutiny of relevance. There was an itch to scrap what was not meaningful to the present day and age. There was a restlessness to be seen to be relevant. Witness was a catch-cry. It was not enough to do things: they had to be seen to be done. We had it in Maynooth College. I remember the student council organising a march to the British Embassy from the College to protest about the killings of the thirteen on Bloody Sunday in Derry. There was the strong feeling that this heady protest was a spiritual and moral duty. You had to be hungry and have swollen feet and be jaded from six hours of walking and standing and there had to be a press release or we were not really relevant to the immediate needs of the present time. It wasn't a sufficient response to go the the chapel and pray about such an atrocity

Michel Quoist's prayers are a typical example of this mood. He was forty when the Vatican Council opened. Trained in sociology, he worked as assistant priest in a large working-class parish at Le Havre. He was appalled by the 'awesome problem of social injustice' as he called it and by 'the untold suffering everywhere in the world.' And so his prayers are not 'composed' as such, they are colloquial. Indeed, he has intimated that they were written from jottings made from problems which came his way in the presbytery parlour: 'Prayer before a £5 note', 'The Tractor', 'The Telephone', 'The Brick', 'Housing', 'The Hospital', 'The Delinquent.' Each prayer grows from a problem.

These strip away the formalism and pharisaism of a lot of conventional prayer. Some of them even shock us into relevance like 'The Pornographic Magazine.' Many priests as well as seminarians who had becomes tired of their own superficial praying were galvanised into prayer with these compositions. Their great value was to show people that the ordinary daily events are relevant to God and we should pray about them in spontaneous words. God often speaks to us through young protesters, Quoist believes, even when they are unfair and strident, because 'they shake us out of our habitual complacency and our self-satisfaction with our way of thinking and a life-style which we no longer question sufficiently'. The workers' lives whose homes he shared break into his prayers all the time.

I have eaten
I have eaten too much . . .
While at that moment, in my town, more than 1,500 persons
queued up at the bread line . . .
Lord, it's you who queue up at the breadline,
It's you who eat the scraps of garbage . . .
Lord, it isn't easy to feed the world.

I would rather say my prayers regularly, properly;
I would rather fast on Fridays . . .
But apparently that isn't enough.
It's nothing, if one day you can say to me: 'I was
hungry.'

Or on housing:

Lord I can't sleep: I've got up out of bed to pray.
It's night outside and the wind blows and the rain
falls.
I know that in one single room 13 people are
breathing on one
another . . .
I know that the rats come out to eat the crusts and
bite the babies.
I know a drunken father who vomits on the child
sleeping
beside him.
I know hundred of others — yet I was going to sleep
peacefully
between my clean-white sheets.

Or in the hospital:

Lord, suffering disturbs me oppresses me;
I don't understand why You allow it.
Why, Lord? Why this innocent child who has been
moaning for
a week, horribly burned?
Why this suffering in the world that shocks, isolates,
revolts, shatters?'

And yet, in spite of the pathos and poignancy of such
utterances we seem to have now outlived the relevance phase
of active life spilling into prayer. It has given way, more or
less, to what I call the third phase, the craving for 'authenticity.'
Now we have to be authentic. We are less concerned with being
seen to be relevant as with searching our heart of hearts —
making the journey inward which I mentioned at the outset.
This is having tremendous effect on present styles of prayer.
We are discovering, as if for the first time, that God is not 'in

the storm' or in 'the mighty wind' but in 'the gentle breeze.'
We are doing no more, perhaps, than endorsing Augustine's
discovery of *Deus intimior intimo meo*: God is closer to me than
I am to myself.

This, one could say, is the central theme of practically all
popular spiritual writers at the present time: René Voillaume,
Carlo Caretto (both strongly inspired by the desert spirituality
of Charles de Foucauld), Edward Farrell, Jean Vanier, John
Dalrymple, George Moloney, Peter Van Breeman, Henri
Nouwen, Thomas Green, Thomas Merton, Adrian Van Kaam:
all of these stress in their various fashions and from different
angles that the journey to God is a journey inward as well as
outward. We are recognising that our problem now is, not that
we take refuge from action in spiritual things as might have
been the case in the pre-conciliar Church, but that we are
strongly inclined to hide altogether from spiritual things.

Action without roots can be an escape and a distraction.
Busyness can become a welcome anaesthetic to numb our inner
ache for peace. We are afraid of relaxing into God: we dread
the pain of self-discovery. Keep going, that's the impulse. Yet
it amounts simply to distraction, and contributes to a feeling
of lostness.

There is, I think, a graphic image which can be applied to
such a sense of being lost in *The Second Coming* of W.B. Yeats:

> Turning and turning in the widening gyre
> The falcon cannot hear the falconer;
> Things fall apart; the centre cannot hold;

Things will fall apart in a priest's life if he has no centre. He
will go on turning and turning in an every-widening gyre
precisely because he has stopped hearing the Falconer Christ.
We celibates have to think continually about this. Unlike
married men who cannot forget the centre of their lives, a wife
and children, we celibates who are not tethered to a partner
in marriage can lose our direction according as we lose touch
with Christ. Many priests and religious who became, sometimes
frantically, over-involved in the social plight of people after
the Vatican Council found it difficult to keep recognising God
in their brothers and sisters, because they had lost the habit
of discerning him in themselves.

They ended up finding only themselves or their brothers and sisters. It frightened many and caused some to panic. The slow spiritual salvation resulting from one-sided dedication to action began to make itself felt more and more insistently, as hunger always does in a basically healthy person until a certain critical threshold is reached. Hunger strikes have revealed that prolonged abstinence from food can actually create a revulsion for it. It becomes eventually impossible to eat, because food becomes the most sickening sight for the hunger striker. What is verified on the physical plane is sadly true on the spiritual too. Prayer after a long period of neglect can become unpalatable, even impossible. At that point the activist can either drift away from God and religion altogether, or he can make what I might call the 'inward turn', the turn back to contemplation which is the return to the living roots of all fruitful action. Many energetic and generous people dedicated to Christian social action have begun to feel the need to take time out from their action, from their *working for God* in their brothers and sisters, to turn within and seek his own face directly as he dwells in his own unique and mysterious personal reality within them; in a word, *to live with* him in mutual presence.

Because the dominant thrust of our spirituality after the Vatican Council was outward — very sincere and generous as it was — it could cause the priest a crisis of self-identity and self-confidence. Catapulted by concern into frenzied action, many felt their inspiration dry up. Yet, if we priests feel such a pinch, it is a crisis in which we ought not to panic but see as an invitation to renew ourselves at a deep level; rooting our actions in the silent seedbed of contemplation, making the journey inward. But the beginning of the journey is irksome!

Monica Furlong once had a letter from a friend serving a long prison sentence. She wrote:

The time is now 9.30 and I've just been locked up. You may find this difficult to understand, but I find this period the best part of the day.

If I could only somehow discipline myself to spend the *opening-up* period in my cell I'm sure I'd be able to to be a more stable person. But I find as long as my door is open, I cannot voluntarily spend much time in my cell . . . . If I am not wandering around I feel I will miss something . . . .

Unfortunately, we all prefer to dodge the call to empty ourselves out, to return to our roots in stillness. Yet a good priest is a man who does not just reach out in contact, nor measure himself by what he achieves. Movement and mission will be vain gestures beating the air, if they do not derive from an inner depth, reflection and love. Considerations of achievement are secondary. He is called to be *with* the Lord and then to be *sent out*.

Charles Davis, one of the first sensational departures from the priestly ministry, very honestly confessed on one occasion that he was so busy theologising about God that he had not time to talk *to* God!

Shortly before leaving the priesthood some years ago he said:

Much speaking in different places on themes of renewal has brought me into contact with many people seeking to revivify their faith. I have found a sense of emptiness, but together with it a deep yearning for God. There is an emptiness at the core of people's lives, an emptiness waiting to be filled. They are troubled about their faith; they find it slipping. I am not speaking of those who are worried about recent changes. These people are not. But they are looking for something more; they are looking for something to fill the void of their lives, and what they hear does not do that.

The more perceptive know they are looking for God. He seems to have withdrawn from the world and from them. They come to talks by speakers like myself. They hear about the new liturgy, about the new understanding of the layman's role, about collegiality, about the Church and the world, about a thousand and one new and exciting ideas. They are duly impressed. But who will speak to them quite simply of God as of a person he intimately knows and make the reality and presence of God come alive for them once more?

Before such need, how superficial, pathetically superficial is much of the busyness with renewal. We reformers know so much about religion and about the Church and about theology, but we stand empty-handed and uncomfortable when confronted with sheer hunger for God. Holiness is less easily acquired than fluency in contemporary thinking. But people who, after listening to our enthusiastic discourses, quietly ask us to lead them to God are, though they do not know it, demanding holiness in us. I fear they may find everything else but that . . . . Saints were required in the past to renew the Church. We suppose we can get by as spiritual operators.

Unless we priests are men of deep faith, strongly attached to Christ in prayer, we will stand empty-handed before the people who rightly expect us to have discovered Christ in our lives and to have grown to love him deeply through a personal attachment.

We are tempted to forget that Jesus himself, busy man that he was, stretched to the limit physically and emotionally by the demands of his work, left the sick unhealed, the mourning uncomforted, the ignorant untaught, and stole off by himself to meet with his father in deep prayer.

We pray, as Thomas Merton would put it, not to recharge our batteries to go back to the concerns of daily life, but rather to be transformed by God so that the myths and fictions of our life might fall like broken shackles from our wrists. This is not lost time, for after it our work will go better than ever

We withdraw within not to retreat from life but to retreat from the constant evasion, the constant fearsome retreat from all that is real in the eyes of God. We pray to discover our true self, and through it the real God and the real world.

In this way the false dichotomy between work and contemplation in the priest's life dissolves. Both fit together and dove-tail; they are not mutually exclusive. It is not a question of choosing between the vocation of a recluse or an activist. The Russian writer, Catherine de Hueck Doherty, in her book *Poustinia* (Russian for hermitage), uses a child-bearing image to reconcile the two impulses:

Suppose that you were married and became pregnant. Would you stop cooking for your husband? Would you stop doing the laundry, the cleaning, stop going to meetings on racial justice and school affairs? No. You'd go about your daily business. The only difference between you and everyone else would be that you were carrying a child.

Your womb is a poustinia for the child, and you carry him wherever you go. Wherever you go you are pregnant with Christ, and you bring his presence as you would bring the presence of a natural child. For when a woman is with child, people give her special attention. They smile, they offer her a comfortable place to sit down. She is a witness to life. She carries life around with her.

Applying this example to the mystery of being pregnant with God (and it applies to both men and women), you have, as it were, a *poustinia within you*. It is as if within you there was a little log cabin in which you and Christ were very close; in this attitude you go about your business.

God forbid you should all become recluses or hermits! That is not what is meant by being a poustinik (a hermit) in the marketplace. It means that within yourselves you have made a room, a log cabin, a secluded place. You have built it by prayer, the Jesus Prayer, or whatever prayer you have found profitable.

In a manner of speaking, nothing has changed in your daily schedule. You are not 'retiring recluses.' Far from it! So you attend all the meetings as before, knowing in deep faith and its accompanying darkness that you are bringing Christ, the Christ who prayed to his Father all night, alone on the mountain. You bring the Christ who stole away from the crowds to pray. You are now carrying him back to the crowds. So you should be with the crowds.

I think it helps us to cope with difficulties in prayer if we view it as friendship with God. But we must accept that our prayer will reflect the movement, the ups and downs, of any human relationship. It passes through the usual phases that mark any normal friendship. At first there is hesitancy and uncertainty. We are drawn to someone but unsure of the next move. We'd like to get closer but don't know how best to express ourselves and are frightened of a rebuff. We are like the disciples who wanted to break through to God but weren't sure how to go about it. They asked Christ, 'Lord, teach us to pray.' And he gave them the right words to use.

After our breakthough, when the floodgates of speech are opened and we are so much at ease with a friend, we cannot find enough time to share our feelings, our views, our past experience and our hopes for the future together. Very often, for example, a courting couple have explored their past and formulated their hopes and dreams for the future before ever they come to settle down. In our office of Readings, in the Liturgy of the Word, we, through instalments of God's word, get glimpses of himself, expressions of his love and his hopes for our future. Just as any human relationship is two-way, we express our wonder and joy in the reciprocation of our responsorial psalms. It is interesting that, while these Hebrew songs can be variously categorised, the feature of praise is common to them all. One cannot help pushing the analogy of the courting couple further. As they grow in awareness of each other they express their mutual appreciation by having records played as they talk about their personal lives and share confidences. Invariably these are love songs with the constant theme: 'you are great; you are wonderful, I love you.' The transposition of the psalm is obvious: the psalms are love-songs which help further our growing attachment to God in prayer.

But all human relationships go through a third phase: they

lapse again into silence and if our attachment to God is to be real we must expect it to echo this stage as well. But this time it is an easy and deep silence, for the partners know where they stand with each other. It is a relaxed, not an uneasy, silence. The experience is captured in our old aphorism: 'still waters run deep' and the quieter, the deeper. The mature friendship goes beyond words and rests in the acceptance of mystery. In a French novel by Anne Philipe called *Le Temps d'un Soupir* a wife can say of her husband after several years of shared life:

I am able to finish any sentence that he begins and yet his slightest smile contains more mystery than the Mona Lisa.

An old couple in one of Thomas Hardy's novels has reached such a deep level of love that presence has become everything and in her simple way the wife will not try to capture it beyond saying:

I look up and there he be;
He looks up and there I be.

John Vianney, patron of diocesan clergy, said of his own prayer of eucharistic adoration which lasted in silence for hours at a time:

In this intimate union which prayer is, God and the person are like two pieces of wax, melted together into one, so we do not need to say a lot to pray well. We know God is there. He opens his heart to us. Considering this presence — that's the greatest prayer.

But for this to happen we must work hard at our appreciation of Christ's presence.

One has, however, to be very careful about laying down guidelines for prayer, because it is an expression of relationship and therefore a very delicate and personal expression. As we all know from our experience, in developing a relationship what matters is not technique but attitude. If we begin with longing and love, our individual method will grow out of our love. A readiness to be changed and to share — the marks of true love — as well as humility and trust are all that we need. Too much concern with method will spoil prayer by shifting the focus from God to our personal experience of the process of prayer. Preoccupation with method will make us more conscious of

what we are *getting out of* our prayer than the wonderful person who is loving us in our prayer, and who is gradually taking us, through our loving surrender, to his level of life and love.

In the eucharist we have the source and meaning of our priesthood. I find it helpful to recall in relation to the eucharist that when Christ speaking in Aramaic took bread he said '*Hu Bishri*. This is *myself*'. The eucharist summed up the entire giving of himself which had been expressed in several different ways throughout his ministry. He had responded to different people by giving sometimes his healing, sometimes his forgiveness, his time, his love and so on. In the eucharist he gave and gives himself completely. His body, yes, but his mind, his strength, his courage, his peace as well. When he used the word 'blood' as he lifted the cup he was again saying 'I give you *myself*' because for the Hebrews 'blood' means a man's whole life. It is the entire Jesus, the Risen Lord, then, who is present to us in a living, dynamic way in the eucharist, and the words 'body' and 'blood' in our language may fail to convey this fulness, may sound lifeless or inert. That is why I like the sharp expression of the Monaghan poet Paddy Kavanagh when he says:

> For God is not all in one place, complete
> Till hope comes in and takes it on His shoulder —
> O Christ, that is what You have done for us;
> In a crumb of bread the whole mystery is.

Our prayer is mature only when it reaches this level of peaceful awareness and love of God. It is a 'knowing' without knowing, a 'seeing' without seeing, a 'touching' without feeling. It is a surrender in love and it does not need words. In fact words can be a troublesome distraction; they can even keep people apart: we talk about the weather often because we're uncomfortable about sharing ourselves. This truth has been well portrayed in a fine film called *The Heart is a Lonely Hunter*. In it the hero, a deaf mute, strikes up a strong relationship with a young lad of his own age who has befriended him and who, every week, takes him out of the institution where he is looked after and brings him to play football and enjoy a good, home-cooked meal. The deaf mute invariably breaks down and cries when he is being brought back to the hospital, and you can sense the deep friendship that has developed even though one of them can neither speak nor hear.

In the same film other relationships are contrasted. A teenage boy and girl, both very attractive physically, have a sexual relationship which is obviously shallow and selfish. They seem to use each other but have no commitment or stability. The attachment dissolves as quickly as it springs up. It appears as if the couple fall in love with each other's qualities; there is not true meeting of hearts. They talk a lot but their words are barriers, for they become an excuse for deep communicating; they are misused. We can similarly keep talking to keep God at a safe distance in our 'prayer.' We can be afraid of silence; afraid of receiving him. Just before her death, Thérèse of Lisieux was confined to bed in the infirmary of her convent. To relieve the monotony for her a sister working nearby used occasionally chat to her. One day she asked, 'Thérèse, what are you doing?'

'I'm praying,' Thérèse replied.

'What are you saying?,' the sister asked.

'Nothing,' came the reply. 'I'm loving him.'

Understandably we get restless for rules and method in our prayer, but it is a process as mysterious as opening up in human relationships and it needs as much time. A husband, saying 'the few words' at his golden jubilee wedding dinner and with an unusually happy married life behind him, confessed: 'We've been together for fifty years, we've had a lovely relationship, but I'm afraid she's still a mystery to me!' Prayer, too, is about living patiently with the opaqueness of God, the jealous lover, being simply present to him in love, patiently accepting his mystery.

In *The Edge of Sadness*, a novel about a priest in a busy parish who through depression ends up an alcoholic, the central character, Fr Kennedy, did not bother spending too much time with the Lord. Prayer and preparation for liturgical functions were activities he fitted in if there happened to be any time left over from other more pressing involvements. He gradually convinced himself that work was his prayer and that priestly work was all that was necessary. But he eventually described his own alarming situation in these words.

What he (i.e. a priest) may not see is that he stands in some danger of losing himself in the strangely engrossing business of simply 'being busy.' And gradually, too, he may find that he is rather uncomfortable whenever he is not being busy. He may find fewer and fewer moments in which he can absent himself from activity, in which he can be alone, can be silent, can be still, in which he can reflect and pray . . . . The loss of such moments is grave and perilous . . . . Something within him will have atrophied from disuse, something precious, something vital. It will have gone almost without his knowing it, but one day in a great crisis, say, he will reach for it and it will not be there.

A priest in a parish must take care to find time to be alone, to be still, to be silent, to let himself pray and reflect on his life. It is strange that the busy priest, no matter how busy he is, always seems to be able to squeeze more people into his time, but unfortunately the last person to get squeezed in is often the Lord himself. If you do not offer Christ prime time, if he is not top of your list of appointments every day you are heading for trouble. The Lord always seems to be at the end of the line waiting to be seen, waiting to be heard by the feverish character who is so busy taking care of the Lord's people. This brings to mind the cautionary words uttered at Maynooth by Pope John Paul II himself.

A constant danger with priests, even zealous priests, is that they become so immersed in the work of the Lord that they neglect the Lord of the work. We must *find* time, we must *make* time, to be with the Lord in prayer. Following the example of the Lord Jesus himself, we must always go off to some place where we can be alone and pray. It is only if we spend time with the Lord that our sending out to others will be also a bringing of him to others.

The priest who constantly performs to the applause and approval of the audience out front can tragically forget the ultimate backstage presence of God.

Most of us have noticed the large number of married women who complain that although everybody around thinks their husbands are great because they devote a lot of time to good work helping others, the tragic irony is that these men find little or no time for their wives, the one person in their lives for whom they should have been able to find time. Marriage intimacy breaks down if the couple have no caring time for each other apart from their involvements together. I have seen it introducing strain, in the best of marriages, even where the couple are involved in excellent apostolic movements such as Marraige Encounter, which is itself directed towards improving the quality of married life for others.

The same holds true for the priest's attachment to the Lord. Celibacy is not some kind of penitential burden that priests are asked to tolerate as a price to pay for their priesthood. The magnificence of celibacy is that it is a gifted and privileged presence, which I experience, which can open me and afford me time to be with Christ. My celibacy frees me for a very active involvement with people in my day-to-day caring for their needs. But if I am not able to discover the Lord's presence in myself, then I am living in a fool's paradise, and the precious something which will have died within me is the intimate experience of his closeness.

Diocesan priests can spend endless hours discussing this loss in their lives and the need to repair it. They insist that they are not monks and, of course, they are not; but many are blind to the inconsistency that though they claim that the Lord lives in others, they are not open to that living presence in themselves.

When I make time for private prayer, which is apart from my work with people, I have to begin by facing the question of whether I can face myself in my aloneness. Can I be still? Can I be silent? Unfortunately many never get beyond this initial problem; they cannot break the boredom barrier. Am I attached to my activities because they serve to protect me from the painful discovery of my own inner emptiness? The superficiality that results from inner emptiness of this kind was well summed up by Thoreau when he wrote: 'In proportion as our inward life fails, we go more constantly and more desperately to the post-office. You may depend upon it, that the poor fellow who walks away with the greatest number of letters proud of his extensive correspondence has not heard from himself this long while.'

We cannot survive on mere outreach. In every priest's life there must a personal time and place for prayer, a personal desert moment in which he becomes daily aware of an interior stillness, an ability to pull himself together and be really present not only to himself but to the Lord. He should not have to have a breakdown or suffer from alcoholism to realise that finding regular time to go apart is important — as happened to the priest in *The Edge of Sadness* quoted above. He captured the effect on himself at the retreat house where he was sent to recover; it was out in a wilderness.

Driving back to the Cenacle at night, passing through the strange quiet and clear darkness of the desert night, I would suddenly become aware of a stillness which was something quite apart from the stillness of the night.

It was an interior stillness, a stillness inside me, a stillness in which there was the absence of all distraction and unrest, a stillness in which, quietly and without effort, I seemed to come together, to be focussed and attentive, to be really present, so to speak, a stillness from which it seemed natural, even inevitable, to reach out, to pray, to adore ... at last I came to terms with myself and with God.

Making the journey inward, then, depends not only on a decision but on physical conditions. We need help, physical helps. We need to choose a congenial setting, Besides, we have to recognise that our bodies affect our minds. We cannot separate the two: we are all of a piece. Unfortunately Cartesian dualism has for too long affected our spirituality and bedevilled our notion of prayer. Most of us were brought up to think of our souls as imprisoned in our bodies. We felt we should deny our bodies in prayer, pray in spite of them, and certainly not be comfortable in prayer. There is always need for self-denial, but there is need, too, for an acceptance of our bodies in prayer. We *are* our bodies, we do not just inhabit them. A lovely experience in Jerusalem helped me in this. I was in a little monastery chapel when Abyssinian monks were assembling for prayer. As each man reached his choir stall he took up a long crutch, placed it under his left arm and leaning on it began his prayer. At first I thought they were a community of invalids, but no, they were all hale and hearty. It is simply their expression of what communion in prayer ideally is: leaning on God.

In the East the normal position for prayer is sitting cross-legged for long periods. This bodily position has an important effect on prayer because with it the breathing changes; it becomes deep and rhythmic. You feel after a while that you *are* your own breathing and you reach a point of concentration very quickly.

Establishing rhythmic breathing like this is a support in prayer which we have lately learned from the East: breathing in as the symbol of silently inhaling the Truth in love and breathing out as the symbol of the active expression of the richness we have assimilated. Whatever form we use, whether it be some such newly discovered technique, a renewed devotion of the past or a revitalised traditional method, it must be marked by a clear focus on the person of Christ as our Saviour, the mediator between God and man through whom we approach the Father by the power of the Holy Spirit.

St Ignatius of Loyola, in his *Spiritual Exercises*, tells us that when we begin to pray we should try one position and if that is not satisfactory we should change it until we find one that suits us better. In practice, positions vary greatly for people of different ages, places and cultures. In a Church elbows on knees and feet on kneelers may be best. In a small chapel with flat cushions we may find that the ideal position is sitting cross-legged on the floor with our backs free or supported against the wall. For some people outstretched hands is a helpful gesture; it is a continuing reminder of our own emptiness and that only when we admit our need can God begin to fill it. Kneeling up helps engender attitudes of adoration and reverence.

Prone on the floor is a favourable position for maturing a sense of smallness in relation to God, or the sensation of surrender and helplessness which disposes us for true communion with him. To some it is dramatic, but interestingly it is one of the preferred postures for private prayer used by our Holy Father Pope John Paul. What matters is not the position but how it alerts us to meet God in peace, freedom and comfort. Physical disposition is so vital. For example: you hear people say, 'If only I had the time I'd sit down and write that article, or review or letter or homily . . .'. They do not realise it is the sitting down that is the hard bit; creating the physical conditions is the greatest part of the problem. Giving yourself is the beginning of prayer — starting the journey inward.

Pastoral work and prayer

Between prayer and pastorate there is often a puzzling polarity. While in theory none of us advocates an other-worldly piety, we diocesan priests can in practice end up divorcing our prayer from our pastoral activity. Prayer and work collide and seldom coalesce. And the result is a mutual impoverishment. It is possible to read the breviary piously, celebrate daily Mass and preserve our celibate condition by remaining cocooned from the plight of people, being convinced all the while that we are unassailably fulfilling our ministry. But unless our spirituality finds issue in a dynamic service of people, and unless the sufferings and joys of those we serve 'break into' our prayer-life, we are 'compartmentalising' our priesthood. What we need is an integrating overview.

The teaching of the Second Vatican Council helps us acquire this. Particularly with its stress on the priesthood of lay people, it de-emphasises the priest belonging to a caste apart. It places him squarely among the people he serves. While he prays for them, they must pray with him. He leads them, he proclaims and explains the Gospel and helps people discern Christ in their lives. As Christ's representative he builds up the Church and he does so by healing, reconciling, strengthening and criticising in Christ's name the activity of people who are discerning and worshipping God in the light of the Gospel. He is called by the Church to draw the people together in the power of the Gospel and into the unity of the eucharistic celebration.

We are indebted to biblical scholarship which has, particularly since the Second Vatican Council, investigated the rich background which the New Testament provides for a deeper understanding of priesthood. Raymond Brown, for example, advises that four different strands interweave to provide the inspiration, motivation, and dedication which should be associated with the priest.

The first and basic quality is that of the *disciple*. It suggests an intimacy and familiarity with Christ. It also implies a readiness to share generously with others whatever we have derived in terms of learning or experience from the Lord's company. The second strand of influence shaping the priest's role is that of the *apostle*. The notion of apostleship, as we all realise, means being sent to work for others in the name of Christ, spreading the knowledge of his message and making his mission effective. A further development occurred with the emergence of the residential *presbyter-bishop*, whose service is directed towards a settled congregation and who tries to be an 'example to the flock' through his teaching, administering and caring. As time passed he assumed the role of *president at the eucharistic assembly* and gradually the Church saw its life focussed on the eucharistic celebration and on the preaching of the Word, which gather together the 'Church'.

An exclusively cultic priest, a 'sacristy priest' who lives apart from his people is not, therefore, being true to the genuine tradition of the priesthood. The strong conventional view of priestly spirituality which somehow separated ministry and spirituality by implying that the priest stores up spiritual energy in his prayers and then expends that energy in his apostolate has been greatly altered or at least enlarged by both Vatican II and the Synodal document on priesthood. The thinking of these documents breaks that dychotomy by stressing that the priest's ministry is the prime source of his spirituality. Through his ministering to people he is sanctified.

Every priest will find in his very vocation and ministry the deep motivation for living his entire life in oneness and strength of spirit. Called like the rest of those baptised to become a true image of Christ, the priest, like the apostles, shares besides in a special way companionship with Christ and his mission . . . . Therefore in the priestly life there can be no dychotomy between love for Christ and zeal for souls.

Modern theology of priesthood, therefore, which is based on the Council documents, tends not to stress the traditional notion of *ex opere operato* because that principle can encourage a division in the priest's life between his work and prayer. Not only can it make his work mechanical and perfunctory but it can distract the priest from the fact that his own pastoral work is meant to be a rich and essential source of spiritual growth to himself. What the document on ministerial priesthood is saying is that the priest is not a kind of instrument changing other people while being unaffected by this work in his own personal spirituality. When we think about it, this makes good sense. Personal prayer is essential to create the sensitivity, the living faith that helps us see Christ at work, through our ministry, in the lives of people. The priest-poet, Gerard Manley Hopkins, captures beautifully this aspect of the mystical body in his lines:

Felix Randal the farrier, O is he dead then? my duty all
    ended
Who have watched his mould of man, big-boned and hardy-
    handsome
Pining, pining, till time when reason rambled in it and some
Fatal four disorders, fleshed there, all contended?

Sickness broke him. Impatient, he cursed at first, but mended
Being anointed and all; though a heavenlier heart began some
Months earlier, since I had our sweet reprieve and ransom
Tendered to him. Ah well, God rest him all road ever he
    offended!

This seeing the sick endears them to us, us too it endears.
My tongue had taught thee comfort, touch had quenched thy
    tears,
Thy tears that touched my heart, child, Felix, poor Felix
    Randall.

Without deep personal prayer we lose awareness of God's grace, we lose faith in his presence in others, 'For God goes by with quiet footfall.' Mother Teresa reminds us that there is only one Christ and if we do not regularly love him in the Eucharist we will not have eyes to recognise him in our needy brothers and sisters, and by the same token, if we do not serve him in his broken members, we are hypocrites when we approach his eucharistic presence. So, priestly prayer and ministry are all of a piece. We are spiritual schizophrenics if our prayer life is not fed by our active life, and our private prayer life is barren if it is segregated from our pastoral ministration. Priests who practise the poverty of availability, who are generous in responding to people's needs, are enriched as priests in a deep, spiritual way. They find that the demands of people frame their priestly identity. The expectations of people bring out the best in them and constantly remind them of the purpose of their priesthood. If a priest reacts to this stimulus he becomes more and more conscious of what it is to be a priest and a steward of the mysteries of God.

Devout little people in his care keep revealing to the priest the mystery of the faith — if he has eyes to see. They frequently share their devotion with him — if he has ears to hear. I remember Paddy McGee, a bedridden old man who had lost both legs, time and again breaking into tears and crying with joy when I brought him holy communion. Paddy had never missed Mass in all kinds of weather when he was fit to walk, and even when unable to climb the steps to the Cathedral, he had gone as far as the gates and gazed up while Mass was being celebrated so deep was his devotion to the eucharist. The way he prayed his thanksgiving in his invalid bed warmed my heart to the presence of Christ. Coming away I felt that I had not visited Paddy but rather he had visited me; or, more truly, Christ had visited both of us.

Again a remarkably devout nun, who revived while being anointed by a hospital chaplain, alerted him to the wonder of his ministration by remarking: 'Remember, father, it's a sacrament you're giving me.'

A beautiful young girl Josie, an art teacher who was confined to her hospital bed, recalled to me what her feelings were the day she first heard she was suffering from multiple sclerosis and would never recover. It would be just a matter of months till she was confined to bed for the rest of her life, able to move only her eyes and her head a little until she died an early death. It was a fight against anger which she won. She came out of the protracted struggle with an urgent plan for the short life left her. She told me she knew she had a vocation and whatever happened she was determined to see it through. It was a vocation to do the Father's will as Christ did, she said, except that the cross she was nailed to was a bed. She lives with the realisation that in every passing *now* she has all the time there is in the world and only one thing to do with it, his will. Nothing has changed her more than this limitation of herself to each moment that is given her. Just making the absolute most of it. God has overturned her plans and revealed to her the preciousness of time as an opportunity to simply give herself to him. It's ten years since I met her and her final words have never left me: 'I'm not fit to get up and go up to mass but' she said, trying to rub her hand on the bed, 'I think I'm suffering my own mass on this altar.' Ever since, as I repeat Christ's words at mass, 'This is my body which will be given up for you,' and try to make them a summary of my own life, I cannot help admitting that I learned from her how my words at mass must become flesh and absorb my entire life.

This deepening awareness of the Christian faith can take place in the most unexpected spots with the most surprising people. As captured by the poet Paddy Kavanagh, farmers working in a ploughed field on a raw March day can have eyes to see, when the sun comes through a gap,

> God the Father in a tree;
> The Holy Spirit as the rising sap
> And Christ the green leaves that will
> Come at Easter from the sealed and
> guarded tomb.

With the present-day trend of encouraging lay people to assume greater responsibility in parish life and be commissioned for the discharge of special ministries in the Church, priests are recognising that many spiritual talents went untapped in the past and our community life is the poorer for that. Indeed the spiritual resources of our lay people remain, largely, an unchannelled potential. Only when we grow less possessive will we enable them to contribute confidently and play their full part as 'a priestly people'. Our greatest mistake would be to imagine that our ministry is a one-way process. Our sense of ministry needs nourishment and we ought never grow apart or aloof from the people we serve. Even the continual respect people show a priest renews his awareness of the 'treasure we hold in common clay pots,' for they salute the office as much as the man.

The trusting way in which people ask for our intercessory prayer, as well as invigorating our own weakness, reminds us of that commitment made in ordination to 'maintain and deepen a spirit or prayer appropriate to our way of life and, in keeping with what is required of us, to celebrate faithfully the liturgy of the hours *for the Church and for the world.*'

People keep reminding us that we are appointed priests on their behalf and that we have the responsibility of bringing their needs with us to prayer. When we pray the Prayer of the Church for the world, we are exercising the mediatorship of priesthood. The high priest Aaron, in case he might forget his continued duty to pray on behalf of his people, always brought the sign of the people on his breast when he went into the Holy of Holies to pray. A priest's breviary, just like his celebration of liturgy, contributes to his own holiness when it is not divorced from his daily activities but in fact expresses what he tries to live day by day. He intercedes for the people but he also shows genuine care and compassion for their needs. He celebrates the sacred mysteries but tries in his life to epitomise the word he preaches and the sacrifice he makes present. Otherwise his celebration is mere ritual and has only shallow significance. He develops spiritually 'through his liturgical ministry only if he stands judged in his own life by the word he proclaims to others and challenged to the same conversion, faith and love that he preaches to his people.'

Another way in which a man's personal spirituality is strengthened through his ministry is by the awareness that God's power is in fact working through him. Most priests at one time or another truly experience that their effectiveness as priests is coming not from themselves but from a power beyond themselves. An old parish priest once remarked to me in a moment of honest soul-searching that the most effective homily he ever preached (in so far as he could judge) was one he was least proud of. He felt disappointed after he had delivered it, ashamed of his 'performance', and yet it was the only occasion in his whole preaching life when a parishioner came around to the sacristy after Mass and confided that God had got through to him when he was ready to despair. I had a similar reaction from a listener abroad who wrote to thank me for the comfort she gained from a radio homily of my own. It came to her,

though, from a throw-away phrase, an incidental point to which I had attached no importance. I felt thanked for something I had not set out to do. It puts us in our place when our main message is overlooked or arouses little reaction by comparison with the tangential. For then God's Spirit is moving not because of us but in spite of us or beyond us.

I think the conferences of the charismatic movement remind us to bring the Spirit of Christ back into our ministry in a more vigorous way. He is already there, of course, but we have to be reminded that when we preach, reconcile, teach, and heal, the love and saving power are from the Lord Jesus Christ. We often forget this. We take over too much and then we worry excessively about our effectiveness. This worry, when we ponder on it, is inverted arrogance, because we are taking to ourselves the ultimate responsibility for priestly work which belongs to the Lord. Unfortunately this is what happens when we do not make our ministry of the Word and our ministry of the sacraments a deep personal prayer as we should. Routine numbs our sensitivity and blunts our awareness of the mystery of Christ's activity on these occasions. A good example is the Ministry of the Word; it ought surely to be an integral part of our own spirituality.

As the liturgy of our commissioning urges, 'In order to carry out their work in a more perfect and suitable way, ministers of the word should meditate carefully on scripture. They should realise the importance of the office they have accepted. They are to make special efforts to develop and deepen a warm and living love and understanding of scripture, and thus become more perfect followers of the Lord Jesus.'

So our ministry begins with pondering in the heart, careful meditation, and then issues forth in our style of living. What happens on the altar, at the ambo, may not be separated from what happens in our hearts, or from the conduct of our lives. We recall the words of Paul: 'I treat my body hard and make it obey me, for fear that I, after preaching to others, should be myself disqualified' (1 Cor 9:27).

Preparing the Sunday homily, therefore, is a weekly opportunity to form ourselves in the Gospel. I know groups of priests who meet weekly to discuss their Sunday homily. One diocesan group meets early in the week and its basic approach is not to start thinking how best to put across a particular point that appeals. It is rather to pray first of all about what the piece of scripture is saying to each priest in the situation of his own life. This is an enriching experience of spiritual growth and the outcome is naturally a more deeply spiritual sermon.

The administration of penance or baptism or the sacrament of the sick should all be occasions integrated into our personal prayer, not divorced from it. They should inspire praise, joy, gratitude when we reflect on how Christ is restoring people through our own hands. Maybe a prayer before we administer baptism or go out to the confessional, that we will open to the mystery of Christ's presence, would make our celebration of each sacrament a deepening of our own personal attachment to him.

Apart from the sacraments, how many opportunities do we let slip for using our priestly power? We are shy about praying with people. We keep our spirituality in our hip-pockets, so to speak. People often bring us to our senses: they surprise us and shame us by their faith in our healing power. 'Pray over me, father' they plead. We readily advise but we hesitate to pray. We should try to join prayer to advice. This, of course, will come easiest to the man who is already committed to a regular pattern of personal prayer. Only someone abandoned to God can bring discernment to each pastoral situation. Merely praying with people cannot substitute. A personal prayer which is only random soon dissolves. What I have in mind is an attempt to wed both work and prayer, allowing ourselves to be touched at a deep level by the sacred mysteries which we handle.

Gaining fulfilment: celibacy

It is extremely difficult for us to accept or even to grasp the paradox which is at the heart of deep priestly fulfilment. It is a gift we receive when in the first instance we make the entire gift of ourselves to God. Our giving is a prerequisite for receiving. The paradox of fulfilment is, I think, well illustrated in the image of sculpture.

When Michelangelo chipped the block of marble, a possibility died with every chip, but bit by bit the Pietà was born. If he had not chipped at the marble block it would have lain to the end of time, full of possibilities but empty of fulfilment. A good choice means growth, but it also means narrowing. To grow into one possibility, I must die to others. Unlike the marble block, it is I myself who must freely choose to die to all but one, or my freedom for all possibilities will become a trap for all my freedom. So long as I try to hold out several possibilities none becomes a reality. We are slow to relinquish options on our lives, but if we could see with the values of God we would see in this narrowing not impoverishment but enrichment. The things we give up for the kingdom, like position, ambition, marriage and money, God is removing from our grasp like a father removing the toys from the hand of a child tired out with distraction so that he may rest more peacefully and securely. It is our own nervous clutter of possessions which renders us unfree, which shackles us. Unfortunately, we cannot always manage to align our point of view with God's. We are prone to the continual fear that as Francis Thompson puts it in *The Hound of Heaven*, 'Lest having Him we must have naught beside . . .'.

I fled Him, down the nights and down the days
I fled him, down the arches of the years.
I fled him, down the labyrinthine ways
Of my own mind, and in the midst of tears
I hid from Him, and under running laughter . . .
For though I know His love, who followed
Yet was I sore adrad.
Lest, leaving Him, I must have naught beside.

Like the story of the pig and the hen — if one may be permitted to move from the sublime to the ridiculous! One day, as a pig and a hen stood by a grocery window contemplating together their contribution to humanity, an argument arose between them. The hen boasted of how invaluable were the eggs she donated for the wellbeing of mankind, cackling with egocentric pride. But the pig had the last word as he highlighted the leg of ham: 'It's all right for you', he declared to the hen, 'for you it's just a passing encounter, for me it's total commitment!' Sadly, for most of us the commitment is far from total, and paradoxically that's where we lose out.

Fulfilment in the service of Christ is a paradox, a seeming contradiction. G.K. Chesterton said of a paradox that it is a truth standing on its head to attract attention! So it is just a reversal, not a contradiction.

This paradox is like chasing a shadow: you cannot catch up with it; the further you step towards it, the more it seems to elude you by just that much. It is the paradox which Christ put in the intractable words: 'He who loses his life for my sake will find it, and he who tries to save his life will lose it.' So long as you try to satisfy just yourself you remain empty, unhappy and ultimately unfulfilled.

These words of Jesus make surrender of options and narrowing a condition of growth, a condition of true life.

The Irish patriot Patrick Pearse put it this way:

For this I have heard in my heart, that a man shall scatter — not hoard;
Shall do the deed of today, not take thought for tomorrow's teen

Shall not bargain or huxter with God or was it a jest
of Christ's?
And is this my sin among men — to have taken Him
at his word?

The 'sin among men', the foolish risk of losing security, involves
an abandonment, a renunciation.

Sylvia Plath, the American poet, describing a person unable
to risk commitment, in *The Bell Jar* captures the sensation very
precisely:

I saw my life branching out before me like the green fig tree in the story.
From the tip of the branch, like a fat purple fig, a wonderful future
beckoned and winked. One fig was a husband and a happy home and
children, and another fig was a famous poet and another fig was a brilliant
professor, and another fig was Ee Gee, the amazing editor, and another
fig was Europe and Africa and South America, and another fig was
Constantine and Socrates and Attila and a pack of other lovers with queer
names and offbeat professions, and another fig was an Olympic lady crew
champion, and beyond and above these figs were many more figs I
couldn't quite make out.

I saw myself sitting in the crotch of this fig tree, starving to death,
just because I couldn't make up my mind which of the figs I would
choose. I wanted each and every one of them, but choosing one meant
losing all the rest, and, as I sat there, unable to decide, the figs began
to wrinkle and go black, and, one by one, they plopped to the ground
at my feet.

The fearful person, the passive person, the indecisive person,
the wavering person ends up an unhappy person, an unfulfilled
person, a fragmented person. Trying to keep all options open,
we realise none of them.

We forge our future by a commitment. Otherwise, if we face
it passively we are letting it be determined by everyone and
everything except ourselves.

A commitment enables us to take control of our lives. We
shape them by the goals we set ourselves. A goal which we really
want gives a focal point to our lives because as our lives unfold,
we evaluate all the opportunities that come our way in the light
of our goal: we accept some and reject others, depending on
how they help us achieve that goal.

This poise or equilibrium which generates true, inner freedom
and peace is evident in the words T.S. Eliot put on the lips

of the Archbishop Thomas Becket for his famous Christmas sermon in *Murder in the Cathedral*. Revealing a hint of his own impending murder, he says:

Reflect now, how Our Lord himself spoke of peace. He said to his disciples, 'Peace I leave with you, My peace I give unto you.' Did he mean peace as we think of it: the kingdom of England at peace with its neighbours, the baron at peace with king, the householder counting over his peaceful gains, the swept hearth, his best wine for a friend at the table, his wife singing to the children?

These men, his disciples, knew no such things; they went forth to journey afar, to suffer by land and sea, to know torture, imprisonment, disappointment, to suffer death by martyrdom. What, then, did he mean? If you ask that, remember then that he said also, 'Not as the world gives, give I unto you.' So then, he gave to his disciples peace, but peace not as the world gives. . . .

Jesus found not peace on a cushion but on a cross. It was not shallow, sweet or sentimental. The archbishop rightly refuses to equate the fulfilment offered by Jesus with material peace. Such outward expressions are no more than precarious props. They cannot guarantee or replace spiritual satisfaction.

Celibacy
One specific area of a priest's life which bears out this paradox of fulfilment is celibacy. The challenge of celibacy is a challenge to love at a deep and genuine level: the level of giving. It is not meant as a frustration of our capacity for loving contact; that is to radically misunderstand our call. But it takes a strong person to live celibacy as it should be lived; it takes a healthy and balanced person to prevent celibacy stunting his emotional growth and personality development. Celibacy imposes a burden which emotionally immature people cannot accept without detriment to themselves. In extreme cases they are driven to either seclusion or clinging contacts. To withdraw in cold remoteness, to stifle warmth and tenderness is as unfortunate as emotional dabbling in everybody's life to find some superficial satisfaction and so compensate for our own lack of commitment.

Choosing celibacy is not a flight from life and love. For Christ it was very much a flight into life at its fullest. He was truly sucked into the storm, the strain and the stress of living. So true celibacy cannot be a rejection of love or limitation of a man's power to love but a readiness to respond generously in love and to keep extending that response until, if possible, it is as total, as unselective and as all-embracing as the love of Christ. Men who grow gruff, cold and unloving, who withdraw to safety from the threat of friendly relationships, somehow warp themselves. They fail to relay in their priesthood the gentle love of Christ. Celibacy is not meant to create a vacuum in a man's life by removing marriage. Christ would abhor that. Christ the full-blooded man, gentle but full or fire, sympathetic but strong.

If the following of Christ in his celibacy is simply seen as some anaemic imitation of his bachelorhood it will not not bring fulfilment. It is an acceptance of a responsibility to love and cherish everyone — particularly the unloved and the most needy. And this is the pain which brings peace.

Bachelorhood, we all know, may be nothing more than the selfish avoidance of responsibility. Christ was celibate not because he avoided marriage but because he was completely dedicated to the mission of saving all men, a task which demanded freedom from family responsibilities. Jesus asked: 'Who is my mother and who are my brothers?' and stretching out his hands towards his disciples, he said: 'Here are my mother and brothers.' In other words, 'These are my family ties.'

Jesus was broadening his family to embrace everyone without exception; he wasn't narrowing his capacity for commitment. His family would include everyone. It would not be a wife and a few children engaging his undivided attention. If the married man indulges his attraction to a particular woman by settling down with her for life, the celibate who has equal loving powers freely chooses, in imitation of Christ, to accept responsibility for loving everyone in his care without prejudice to attractive qualities: he is to love indiscriminately.

Of course, the actual experience of celibacy only approximates to the ideal. The same is true of marriage. A movement like Marriage Encounter is today revealing dimensions of this sacrament which are seldom explored or lived. The person who enters either state brings individual defects of character which neither marriage nor celibacy will automatically remedy. Both states embody responsibilities which may highlight these personal problems. For example, the father of a family may be faithful to his wife, he may support his children financially and they may not want for anything. He then feels justified in his belief that he is an exemplary husband and parent, even though his wife does not experience any real companionship from him, and he may even be harsh and careless in the home.

In a film called *The First Snows of Spring* we see this precise truth illustrated. A wealthy father spends money lavishly on his only son, sending him on expensive skiiing holidays. Yet the son remains lonely and frustrated in a hunger for love. His father never allows him to get to know him, never spends time with him, yet does not seem to understand why the boy remains unhappy. So too the priest. The mere fact that he is celibate is no guarantee that his life is that of an apostle or that his celibacy is effective in his particular living of it. In fact everything in his life may belie the promise of his celibacy. This will occur more easily when a man sees celibacy as an imposition of Church law rather than an entire way of life to which he has generously pledged himself.

If a priest adopts a minimalist mentality, if he sees celibacy as a law rather than an opportunity, then the values which his celibacy represents will be neutralised by types of eccentricity and worldliness which the law does not explicitly cover — selfishness, ambition, expensive and time-consuming hobbies and greediness. These are the stock compensations of the celibate. But the generous call which celibacy does represent is answered through being free for people; being at the disposal of those in need of our care, our interest, our guidance, our advice and our assistance; genuine service; the renunciation of success and achievement; surrendering our own rights, wishes, attractions and inclinations; imitation of the helpful way Jesus had with people; his attitude towards settling down and owning property; using whatever we have to help others in need and those in our care; and an attitude of calm and freedom from worldly cares.

Celibacy is the sign of a man who has built his life completely and exclusively on God, of a man responding to the full demands of Christ. He is not content to go half way in his service; he gives till and when it hurts. When we fail to respond fully to the call of celibacy we follow the escape routes I indicated above. One is the option of cold and selfish withdrawal. The other is to take the butterly approach — failing to face and accept our own deep loneliness, which is part of being human, and instead dabbling in relationships with the false expectation that companionship can remove that basic loneliness which is part of our nature. As celibates we often mistakenly feel that there is something wrong if we feel lonely; that we have made the wrong choice in undertaking priesthood or religious life and that marriage will remove our loneliness. Marriage is never a good remedy for that kind of loneliness. Chekhov expressed this when he wrote: 'If you are afraid of loneliness, do not marry.'

Even friendships often flounder from the strain of unreal hopes and craving for a unity which can never be ours. Trying to bypass loneliness with a stagnating closeness only leaves the basic problem waiting to be solved and frustrates the lonely person further. We will get quickly bored with each new friend and contact and we will never persevere in friendship if we fail to come to terms with the loneliness which is an essential ingredient in the make-up of us all. The presence of this loneliness makes sense theologically, it seems to me, when we accept that God posited man as his partner, wanting him to share his infinite love and life. If we are to be capable of a relationship of love with the Infinite God we must be *open to the infinite*. That is how we are made. We are capable of receiving infinity. Because we have that capacity nothing human can go the full way to satisfying it. By our very make-up we are condemned to be lonely and restless.

Nowhere is the sensation better captured than by Evelyn Waugh in his classic novel about a deep friendship: *Brideshead Revisited*:

Perhaps all our loves are merely hints and symbols; vagabond-language scrawled on gateposts and paving-stones along the weary road that others have tramped before us; perhaps you and I are types and this sadness which sometimes falls between us springs from disappointment in our search, each straining through and beyond the other, snatching a glimpse now and then of the shadow, which turns the corner always a pace or two ahead of us.

Augustine, Thomas and John of the Cross have the identical idea. Augustine understood this truth from bitter experience in his famous words about the restless heart: 'You have made us for yourself, O Lord, and our hearts are restless till they rest in Thee.' He only came to appreciate it by the circuitous route of sensual experiment.

I think it helps us to live our celibacy if we accept that our deepest longing is for a beauty which comes *through* the world, but which we cannot manage to possess here and now. We have to be careful about jumping to the conclusion that we will automatically remove loneliness and find happiness by walking away from celibacy or taking up a new job. Such short-circuiting can lead to even deeper frustration. The things 'in which we thought the beauty was located will betray us if we trust to them: it was not *in* them, it only came through them, and what came through them was longing . . . they are not the thing itself: they are only the scent of a flower we have not found, the echo of a tune we have not heard, news from a country we have never yet visited' (C.S. Lewis, *The Weight of Glory*).

In a way, then, our loneliness if viewed from the standpoint of eternity is a very advantageous, though painful, component in our personality because it keeps us focussed on the very purpose for which we are made. To deny this truth is to live with the illusion that, somewhere, sometime, we will come across the person who will remove our personal loneliness and bring peace to our restlessness. We will persist in the fallacy that we are lonely because we are celibate. But absolutistic expectations of this kind have ruined marriages, because married or celibate, only God can fill the emptiness of our hearts. George Herbert, the English poet, in his poem *The Pulley* expressed this insight by imagining God, at man's creation, deliberately leaving a gnawing ache in his person which would prevent man ever becoming self-satisfied and consequently losing the God in whose image he is made:

> When God at first made man,
> Having a glasse of blessings standing by;
> Let us (said he) pour on him all we can:
> Let the world's riches, which dispersed lie,
> Contract into a span.
>
> So strength first made a way;
> The beautie flow'd, then wisdome, honour, pleasure:

When almost all was out, God made a stay,
Perceiving that alone of all his treasure
Rest in the bottome lay.

For if I should (said he)
Bestow this jewell also on my creature,
He would adore my gifts in stead of me,
And rest in Nature, not the God of Nature:
So both should losers be.

Yet let him keep the rest,
But keep them with repining restlessness;
Let him be rich and wearie, that at least,
If goodness leade him not, yet wearinesse
May tosse him to my breast.

To live with our loneliness as a positive force driving us to
God and ensuring we rely ultimately on his power preserves
our celibacy. It helps us develop a security and an apartness
which our work and life demand and it keeps us from reaching
out, greedy for affection and doomed to the frustration bound
to result. Accepting our loneliness in this spirit and so readying
ourselves for the gift of God we make concrete the paradox
of fulfilment. We give at one level to receive at a still deeper
level: we lose to find.

The price of caring

If it is true that the literature of any age echoes the main preoccupations of its people, there is no doubt that we are a lonely generation, hungry for love and a reason to live. These are the predominat themes in the drama, novels and poetry of recent decades.

Terry, in John Hopkin's television quartet of plays *Talking to a Stranger*, is really the spokesman for her age when she says: 'Why is it so lonely? I want to live in a crowd of ten thousand — and never let one of them go home. I want them round, all round me day and night — loving me.'

There can be no doubt of the crying need which people have at the present time to feel that someone cares for them. The pop stars of the 1960s often spoke with a strange knack of poetic clarity about the emptiness of man's life:

> He's just a nowhere man
> Living in a nowhere land
> Making lots of nowhere plans
> For Nobody.
> Doesn't have a point of view
> Knows not where he's going to
> Isn't he a bit like you and me?
> (Lennon and McCartney)

And they give poignant expression to the widespread loneliness of life:

> I look at all the lonely people
> Eleanor Rigby picks up the rice in the church
> where the wedding has been.
> Lives in a dream.

Waits at the window,
Wearing a face that she keeps in a jar by the door.
Who is it for?
All the lonely people where do they all come from?
All the lonely people where do they all belong?
                    (Lennon and McCartney)

It is a loneliness which exists not only at the personal level:
it pervades society. It is typified by an absence of care, as Edwin
Brock so imaginatively and trenchantly expressed it in *Five
Ways to Kill a Man*.

There are many cumbersome ways to kill a man:
you can make him carry a plank of wood
to the top of a hill and nail him on it. To do this
properly you require a crowd of people
wearing sandals, a cock that crows, a cloak
to dissect, a sponge, some vinegar and one man to
hammer the nails home.
Or you can take a length of steel,
shaped and chased in a traditional way,
and attempt to pierce the metal cage he wears.
But for this you need white horses,
English trees, men with bows and arrows,
at least two flags, a prince and a castle
to hold your banquet in.
Dispensing with nobility, you may, if the wind
allows, blow gas at him. But then you need
a mile of mud sliced through with ditches,
not to mention black boots, bomb craters,
more mud, a plague of rats, a dozen songs
and some round hats made of steel.
In an age of aeroplanes, you may fly
miles above your victim and dispose of him by
pressing one small switch.
    All you then require is an ocean to separate you,
two systems of government, a nation's scientists,
several factories, a psychopath and land that no one
needs for several years. These are, as I began,
cumbersome ways to kill a man. *Simpler, direct, and*

*much more neat is to see that he is living somewhere in
the middle of the twentieth century and leave him there.*

It is interesting that in a recent survey carried out among young
people in Belgium about the first quality they look for in their
adults (particularly in priests and teachers) top of the list was
understanding. Young people want us, above all, to show
understanding, to be compassionate. When you think of it that
was the most remarkable trait of Jesus in his ministry It was
the outstanding quality which shone through not only in his
personal encounters but also when he had to deal with crowds.
We see him refusing to dispatch the multitude until food was
found for them. We see him fatigued by a busy day's preaching,
withdrawing to the other side of the lake only to discover that
the eager people had anticipated his movements and got there
ahead of him. He did not turn them away but at personal
inconvenience responded to their need, for he pitied them; they
were to him like sheep who had no shepherd. It was, however,
an understanding which reached deeper than that: it pierced
the depths of the individual heart. We see him confronted with
women and men who had made a mess of their lives but always
he brings out the best in them, making them conscious of their
own potential, never reducing them to the level of their failure,
never limiting them to the narrow confines of their sin. He
saw the heavens open over the head of everyone in misery:
everyone is God's beloved son or daughter.

I imagine the interpretation given in *Jesus Christ Superstar*
of the deep relationship which grew up between Mary Magdalen
and Jesus must be close to the truth. She had met many men
who had used her but Jesus made her conscious of her worth
and greatness through respect and genuine love. No wonder
she gave up everything to follow him. The song in that musical
which is put on Mary's lips, 'I don't know how to love him',
betokens a response little short of infatuation. We have certainly
fallen far short of the level of Jesus' love and care if we deserve
the stinging lampoon from an Irish novelist, Michael Farrell,
who has a character cry out about priests: 'They hate life, they
hate people like us, they hate love . . . Their love of God simply
must become hatred of life' (*Thy Tears Might Cease*).'

When the woman was caught in adultery, Jesus would not

even look in her direction for fear even a glance would reduce her dignity and compound her shame. Such discretion revealed the depths of his compassion and sensitivity. What our modern courses in pastoral counselling express through such jargon as 'unconditional love' and 'non-possessive warmth' Jesus was practising all the time.

Such modern counselling insights are simply uncovering the attitude of Jesus in his helping way with people. He helped them by his understanding to believe in themselves and so give of their best. Understanding is a way of describing the whole direction of a priest's work. 'Bear one another's burdens and so fulfil the law of Christ' was St Paul's succinct way of putting it.Very often there is nothing more we can do for people than share their pain. There is not a total cure for every broken life we enter; there is not a happy ending for every tragic story we hear. But if we continue as a support for someone struggling to understand himself or his difficulty more deeply, the listening ear we offer, the confidence we place in him, may be all he needs to help him grow and cope.

It is often easier to achieve than we think. I recall the words of a widowed mother who remembered with gratitude how, when her son was dying upstairs, the priest in the parish came in: 'He prayed with me and he cried with me and that helped me through.' A young lad, severely wounded in a shooting incident with the British army, whom I went to visit while he as under army guard in hospital, remarked in astonishment 'I never thought a priest would come to visit *me*' and as a result of that simple act I could see that he was transformed in his own self-esteem.

I remember bringing Holy Communion for the first time to a couple living alone in a farmhouse on the fringe of a rural parish but before I got near the house, the wife, who recognised the priest at a distance, came running over the field to meet me. She caught my hands, broke down and kept muttering something I could not understand. I thought she was deranged and it frightened me. I gathered she had lost her only daughter, a child of four in a tragic agricultural accident, the most grim and gory I had ever come across. It seemed as if it had taken place just minutes before; in fact as she rhymed it over I learned it had happened eight years previously. The relief at seeing the priest was her only consolation. He stood for God's presence in the midst of her chaos — a ray of hope, a signpost in the fog, a link with the next world. A word from the priest did not make what she suffered easy but gave it some meaning. I couldn't help thinking of the words from 'Bridge over Troubled Waters': 'I will ease your mind.' The priest by his sheer presence can effortlessly ease the troubled mind.

All she wanted was the priest to sit beside her and say some word of comfort or a little prayer. Flung in the teeth of calamity his assurance was an assertion of God's unfaltering love, that in spite of catastrophe all is well: that suffering needn't be raw evil nor pain pointless, for God writes straight with crooked lines. The priest's feelings are mixed on an occasion like that: there's poignancy and pathos but deep satisfaction. We feel we are God's link with the broken-hearted, as he binds up their wounds. Through our ministry they are assured that no wound is waste: that now there is only one cross and Christ walks under it with every member of his body. Mostly this assurance is conveyed to people by the priest's readiness to step in and put his shoulder to their load. Through this silent vocabulary a stronger message is spelled and a clearer glimpse is shared of the caring Christ.

But there are two dangers in our priestly caring. We need great poise and control to keep moving in and out of other people's lives at crucial and unstable moments without becoming absorbed by their pain and losing our own independence. The first danger is that we would get so involved as to become part of their problem. A priest, for example, could be so supportive of a lonely wife that he holds her marriage together but because of his understanding and listening manner finds that she is growing dependent on him and is substituting his care and compassion for the love her husband fails to give. The priest, sensitive to such a development, must squarely accept that such emotional attachment will make him part of the problem, and unhelpful in solving it. When this happens somebody else will do it better. It calls for strength to enter disordered worlds with the care of Christ and the gift of our own personalities and at the same time monitor the emotional impact and drain upon ourselves. A great personal stability and a strong relationship with Christ are necessary if we are not

to be flattered by the realisation that someone needs us emotionally and if we are to resist the temptation to keep them dependent on us. It calls, I believe, for the mature warmth of a good mother who does all she can for her children to help them do without her!

In *Lonesome Cities* Rod McKuen captures the lonely feeling of such giving and it must find a resonance in the heart of any caring priest:

Watching children grow is like
threatening ivy to climb the garden wall.
You wait for it to happen
You hurry it along with *love*.
But still you're disappointed
at giving someone life enough
to walk off on their own
and not be carried in your arms.
You never turn your back — not once
and yet one day they've grown apart or taller.

It's all the same.
Polly put the kettle on, we'll all have tea.
Giving love to children
has made us older overnight.

The second danger for us, therefore, is that we would look for a return in our caring; that we would expect reciprocation and recognition. A very generous and busy priest who gives his 'all' to his people once recalled the great wound of ingratitude he received on coming into his bingo hall one night. A row had developed between two women. One claimed she had checked ahead of the other and refused to share the prize. The row developed to involve her neighbours and soon ended up in abuse being hurled at the bingo committee and then the clergy. On looking down the hall the priest recognised a woman, for whom he had bought the family groceries the previous week, vehemently ranting against the priests of the parish. In the midst of the furore he then spotted a young lad on whose behalf he had spoken in court about a month before also complaining about the clergy. In his own words he declared to Jesus Christ he would never again do anything for anyone, he would do it all for the Lord! To cope with gross ingratitide of this kind in our priestly ministry we need a similar perspective in our work of caring.

In the tradition of Russian spirituality we find the perfect features of a caring priest in the lifestyle of the hermit, or poustinik, as he was called. There was no latch on his door; he was always there to welcome anyone who came. There was a gracious hospitality about him. He never gave the impression he was disturbed when anyone came to visit him. He had a welcoming face and seemed to be a listening person, a person of few words. But his listening was deep and there was a feeling that he understood. He consoled and he loved but he did not demand anything from anyone for himself. Even a farmer rushing to get his hay saved before the threatening rain could presume on an immediate response; the poustinik dropped everything and went with the farmer.

Fr James Duff, formerly Professor of Classics at Maynooth College, seems from the account of his biographer, Fr Robert Nash, to have reflected the portrait of the poustinik in his parish in Co. Down.

It is hardly an exaggeration to say that, from the day of his appointment, Castlewellan and its interests and its people became for him a sort of obsession. He was never wholly at ease when he was away from them. On his occasional visits to his sister in Dublin, he would explain that he must hurry home, as 'they' would be wanting him in the confessional or in his house. The people had the impression that they owned him, could turn to him at any time, seeking advice or consolation or material help. He never would leave the Church as long as there was a chance of somebody coming in for confession. Whatever he had was theirs. No visitor came but was received with affection, for he had for everyone the love which he drew upon freely from the heart of Christ.

He listened to all worries but he never spoke of his own. Cardinal D'Alton would come, a neighbouring bishop, or one or other of the several young priests whom he directed, or it might be a little child, or a group of children, or a member of the rougher element of the parish — it did not matter. He was there for only one purpose: to be at the disposal of any who wanted him, for any reason, at any time.

A priest's retreat

The priest's need for retreat

I suppose there is no simpler yet no more engaging picture of a priest's retreat than that captured by St Luke in chapter 10 of his Gospel.

When the seventy returned with joy to Jesus, saying: 'Lord, even the demons are subject to us in your name', he said to them: 'behold I have given you authority to tread upon serpents and scorpions, and over all the power of the enemy; and nothing shall hurt you. Nevertheless, do not rejoice in this, that the spirits are subject to you; but rejoice that your names are written in heaven.'

We remember that Jesus had called them first to be with him and then to be sent out. The company of Jesus had to be cultivated first, because it alone could guarantee them success in their work later on. As he was anchored in God, so his disciples had to be anchored in him. So Jesus hinted again at this now that they had returned to tell him how they had fared on the mission he gave them. They were bouncing with joy and it was easy to be in those heady days close to the Master's side. They were intoxicated with their own success: 'Master, even the demons are subject to us in your name.'

It was the enthusiasm of the newly ordained. It was easy popularity. Everything going so well. Couldn't be better. It was the experience of all of us at the exciting time of ordination when we were first sent out, that the Lord was working his marvels through us. But Jesus, careful not to disillusion or dampen the enthusiasm of his men, went on to direct their attention to the real reason for rejoicing — their names had been written in heaven. God had selected them. It was *God's* choice and they were doing *his* work.

The popularity with people and the showy success were certainly there, but that was dangerous. It could distract a man, it could upset his value-system and he could get his priorities upside down. The tide of emotion would ebb and flow, the barometer of seeming success would rise and fall, but his priests would need more to sustain them than either enthusiasm or success, and that could only be himself — his company. He had called them to be with him. Because only his company would secure them when the tinsel of newness began to tarnish, when ministering became ordinary, when the spectacular became humdrum, when it was easy to lose zest, lose heart. It would sustain when a project failed, when doubt seemed to dart and stab at a man, when depression and disgust became travelling companions, when people were insensitive, when those who earlier had kissed his hands would choose to misunderstand, when to keep plodding on would seem impossible, when a man would grow tired even of himself.

I have in mind a case of a middle-aged priest who decided to leave the ministry and shocked his friends. He shocked them because he had no overwhelmingly convincing reason, nothing which could not be reduced to a disappointment or two with people and the failure of some plans he had for himself. Added up, these experiences could not (to the outsider, at any rate) warrant the step taken. And yet there must be a lesson here: human failure with people and personal disappointment cannot determine the direction of our priesthood. Christ must be the bed-rock. Only in his company will we learn to see his point of view and grasp the meaning of his mission. Only in prayer can we align our vision with his.

In a film rich in symbol called *The Secret*, the stranger, who seems to represent Christ, though Christ is never mentioned, is shown as coming down from a mountain. Maybe it is because a man on a mountain has such a sweep of vision that he can lift his sights above petty squabbling and silly preoccupations of people. In the film he is a tall man who walks with dignity and holds his head high.

The people among whom he walks know he has a great vision which he will not share lightly. To catch it, a man has to climb the high hill *for himself*. Because he went aside to savour in constant prayer the company of the Father, Jesus kept his sights high. He remained the man of vision. That's why we need retreats.

After a few years in the ministry a man may realise that the heroic sacrifice of which he dreamed would consist of the challenge of coping with mediocrity, disappointment, even failure. Jesus was warning his ebullient disciples that the real rewards for ministry would be made by God in heaven and would not be determined by an eagerly receptive congregation here below. 'For', in Paul's pithy expression, 'our lives are hidden with Christ in God.'

'So do not rejoice because the devils are subject to you'; in other words, don't get carried away by an external evaluation of your priestly work. Far too often we weigh our success on human scales. We get depressed and upset because we think we're getting nowhere. We can hope to be no greater than our Master, and his ministry was in his lifetime ostensibly a failure. It would appear to have been purposely unspectacular, unheroic, and his appointment took him, you might say, to a remote wilderness, living with farmers and fishermen who talked about nothing other than threading needles, patching old clothes, filling wine-skins, grinding meals, making bread, catching fish and mending nets. With them he was content to notice such simple scenes as darnel weeds growing in patches of wheat, mustard seeds expanding into shrubs, the hen with her brood of chickens, the ploughman, builder and burglar at their trade. The materials could not be less dramatic, the scene more ordinary; such as borrowing a few loaves of bread at midnight for a friend's supper. He spent his life tramping about in the swamps, the drains and the ditches of our own dark ways, and he does not promise his priests any better.

It is appropriate, I believe, to centre a priests' retreat in that lovely Gospel scene because we too are running back to Christ: what else is a priests' retreat? Like the seventy we confide in him once more. It may not have been all excitement since he first sent us out. We may not now be so starry-eyed as we used. We may have lost some idealism. We may have grown a little hardened or cynical, especially if circumstances have been rough. Some may even have been injured, or have a serious hurt which needs healing. We may be feeling a little faint-hearted, depressed. The vision could have become blurred and our energy as a result might be sapped. We could be losing drive and enthusiasm — but then we might discover it's the kind that Jesus did not consider too important for his first disciples. Jesus may want to share that insight with us now, to restore our peace and give us fresh heart: Isaiah had said to Yahweh, 'You will keep him in perfect peace whose mind is stayed on you'. That is the anchorage which guarantees us stability and the only genuine security.

And retreat is for strengthening it. We come apart to rest awhile in Christ's company, savour his peaceful presence and, above all, let him speak. He will speak, if we have ears to hear, for grace has its times and a time for retreat is a most sacred time for the promptings of Christ's spirit in our hearts. It is a time, too, for great gentleness towards each other, a time for healing. A man might have a worry or a heaviness in his heart, something bothering his soul, disturbing his peace with Christ. And all ought to pray that such a priest will experience healing of heart and mind.

During a retreat we try to let God take over so that we become more effective instruments of his peace to others. St Charles Borromeo says: 'So now if we remove all barriers, he is ready to come to us again at any minute or hour to make his home spiritually within us with all his grace.' Ambrose, the fourth century Latin Father, who was very taken by the image of Christ standing at the door of our hearts, similarly says:

Let your door be open to him when he comes, open your soul, throw open your inmost mind, so that it may see the riches of simplicity, the treasures of peace, the sweetness of grace.

This exhortation is graphically presented by the English painter Holman Hunt in his familiar picture of Christ, the Light of the World. He depicts our Saviour knocking on a door which has no handle on the outside and which represents a man's heart openable only from within.

In the same vein of thought we can remember the lovely saying of John of the Cross: 'God's greatest gifts fall into empty hearts.' So do not clutter your heart: free it. As Jesus invites us back to his side for a few intensive days together, to re-align our vision with his, he is asking us to rejoice because our names are written in heaven. In other words, rejoice and be glad that we were selected. Thank God for the wonder, the privilege, the honour of your special vocation close to his side. I find that the priest who keeps alive a sense of wonder and gratitude for his vocation and always regards it as something greater than himself will remain a happy peaceful man in his priesthood. Think of all the people Christ could have chosen to be with him, and did not. He wanted you in particular. Thank God for that. Praise him. Musing on the wonder and providence of the gift of existence Jean Guitton penned in his *Journal* some lines of awesome gratitude. Thinking of the sheer 'chance' and contingency of the gifts of human life he was moved to an extraordinary level of rapturous thanks. How much more ought the privilege of religious vocation trigger off in our hearts feeling of deep appreciation and gladness. When we consider how many more worthy recipients God could have found and chosen we must be mesmerised by his providential plan for us.

And as for myself, who think I am as solid and substantial as an indestructible solitaire diamond, I am really but the result of very unlikely combinations and crossings in each generation. My parents might have given birth to two hundred and twenty-five billion different individuals, all equally possible. My heredity, my character, my face, my being, all derive fundamentally from absolutely chance meetings. In the tenth of a second or less, I would have been someone else, or not been at all.

When we were prisoners, to pass the time, we amused ourselves by telling each other how our father met our mother. I remember the oddest trivialities providing the circumstances: a smile, a lock of hair, a jest, a glove picked up, a lost train, a look! Our game did not go on for very long because everyone became serious, awed when he realised on what a pyramid of chance he was poised. Existence, sweet and enjoyable existence, is thus woven of improbable threads! And in my view this is what gives it its strangeness, and its attraction.

The tragedy is, we do not always return that deep love, we do not cherish the vocation he offers us. To take it for granted is to place it in jeopardy. And the day we lose our sense of wonder for it, we are beginning to take it for granted. 'Rejoice . . . because your names are written in heaven.'

Directed retreats

Some priests are now finding great value in taking, once in a while, a directed retreat. Many, however, have never had such an experience. Any retreat involves creating space in one's life for God. It means setting up a situation of outer freedom from normal routine so as to move towards a deeper and inner freedom. The purpose is to find God's will more fully and allow his spirit to renew his life.

Preached retreats and directed retreats simply approach the task in different ways. While a preached retreat involves talks given to a group in the hope that they will find stimulus for self-reflection and personal prayer, a directed retreat offers only one talk a day but entails a commitment to generous periods of personal prayer as well as extensive individual guidance.

Through the conversation each day with the retreat-director an individual's awareness of God's working in his life can be helped on a very personal basis. The retreat is, in a sense, made-to-measure! The director who prays for the retreatant each day listens to the account of life presented to him, suggests scriptural passages for prayer and reflection and tries to discern any pattern of unfreedom and of God's call. He encourages the person's surrender to God and helps him weigh his decisions. It would not have to be an annual affair, of course; but an attempt to look seriously and deeply at our spiritual state on a regular basis, is essential. But some form of retreat should be taken annually and the most common is, of course, the preached one.

Asceticism
Occasionally, a retreat might take the form of a pilgrimage. A recent fine film on St Patrick's Purgatory, Lough Derg, reminded us all most evocatively of our rich national tradition of pilgrimage and penance, but also of the strong and rugged features of Patrick's priesthood.

In forcing a physical renunciation of what is inessential in life we sharpen our spiritual focus on what is central, enduring and true. We accept that we can know Jesus only by following in his way — that following his way is a constant movement away from personal gratification to the detachment which relies only on the Father's Will; that his way can spell itself out in aridity, in frustration, in boredom. In addition to accepting the inevitable irksomeness of life we need to undertake voluntary sacrifices, and foremost among these should be fasting, which enables us to bring our bodies into our prayer in a radical way. We glorify God when we control our desires.

We serve him more freely. Through renunciation we manage to release our hold on all that we're attached to — even *our experience* of God! We are toughened to accept God as he is and preserved from adapting his will to our own convenience.

As Keith Miller confesses in *The Taste of the New Wine*:

> I had been a spiritual sensualist,
> always wanting to feel God's presence . . .
> and being depressed when I didn't . . .
> So I tried this praying
> Whether I felt spiritual or not:
> and for the first time in my life
> found that we *can* live on raw faith . . .
> Often the very act of praying this way
> brings later a closer sense of God's presence.
> And I realised a strange thing:
> that if a person in his praying has the *feeling*
> he doesn't need the *faith*.

The painful purgation of a priest like John Powell as graphically set forth in his autobiographical book *He touched Me* bears out this truth that it is sometimes for our spiritual good to be denied the 'consolations of God' for then we are forced to search for the 'God of consolation.' It is deceptively easy to choose a God of convenience. It is terribly easy to opt for God on the spiritual wave of some great enthusiasm but it is the test of true faith to find peace in the dullness and drabness and darkness. It is on the anvil of ambiguity that our fidelity is forged. It is in pain and perseverance that our prayer is purified

And so T.S Eliot can say:

> I said to my soul, be still, and wait without hope,
> For hope would be hope for the wrong thing:
> wait without love
> For love would be love for the wrong thing;
> there is yet faith
> But the faith and the love and the hope are all in waiting.
> So the darkness shall be the light,
> and the stillness the dancing.

It was Paul VI who declared, 'Vocation today means renunciation. It means sacrifice. It means choosing an austere and constant perfection instead of comfortable and insignificant mediocrity. It means to still the flattering soft voices of pleasure and selfishness'.

The priest has no option but to bring himself continuously, as Paul tried, 'into subjection'; he must be put to death with Christ, prayer and fasting marking him off. While the duty to do penance is an inherent part of the call to be a Christian (in all three synoptic Gospels John the Baptist demands repentance because the kingdom is at hand), we priests are reminded that our pastoral effectiveness depends on our own readiness to do penance by prayer and fasting. Certain evil powers, Jesus declared, would be overcome in no other way but through the rigours of fasting (Mark 9:29). We are to be united to Christ at the deepest level possible. Like him we are to be involved in the travails and trials of mankind, because 'to put on Christ' is to become involved. We are to die a little to ourselves so that Christ's life can spread and others live more. We try to become detached so that some others may grow more attached. In this way we try to serve and save the body of mankind. We are called to accept in our bodies a denial which is an eloquent identity with Christ's dying and rising. We deny our own person so that some other personality may become whole. We recognise that what we *are* gives life to what we pray, endorses what we say. Renunciation, then, is not an optional extra in our priesthood. If there is one feature of Patrick's priesthood which needs echoing for the Irish of today it is surely the ruggedness he gained from asceticism.

My favourite image of him is Seamus Murphy's stone statue at Maynooth, three times life-size. He sculpts Patrick from limestone rock, makes him a giant of a man; tough, rugged, solid and durable — a man with a mission. And I believe that the features of Patrick's faith were rock-like features.

A rock is rooted: it's stayed. To have roots is vital. At the age of sixteen he was uprooted when disaster struck his home. He was snatched from a comfortable living, a well-off family, security and good prospects, and brought to the weather-beaten hills of Ireland as a herdsboy. But in his helplessness he discovered his real security, his true strength: God Almighty.

God became his rock of refuge. 'He comforted me as a Father would his son,' Patrick confessed.

A rock is rugged: Patrick had the ruggedness of the rock and reek. He had a rough physique and strange powers of endurance. He had endless courage and energy. (He survived twenty-eight days in the desert when many of his companions were lying half-dead.) Like the rock, Patrick had his spirit shaped and seasoned through exposure. Exposure to hardship when he was kidnapped, to drudgery and a manual labour which went against his grain, along with the discipline he learned to impose on himself, made Patrick a plain but strong character. Consequently he wasn't shaken in any way by the cynicism of friends who ridiculed him for wasting his time on a mission among heathens.

A rock is durable: it stands the test of time well. It ages and tires and creases with the erosion of time, but it endures till the end. It faces calmly the acid tests of life. 'Even in times of snow or frost or rain I would rise before dawn to pray . . .'. At Patrick's heart-core was an intensity of faith developed through persistent prayer. This gave him durability.

A rock is persistent: it is unflinching. And so it can surmount difficulty and pressure. Patrick was persistent until he achieved his end. In over thirty years of non-stop labour and virtually singlehanded he converted and baptised a multitude of Irish people, ordained clergy for them and organised their churches.

Paradoxically, a rock is vulnerable. It will allow its heart to be hewn upon to house and home others, but it can be misused. Patrick was vulnerable. At heart a lonely person, he felt unwanted and isolated. He didn't have understanding friends during his adolescent years and traumatic exile. He was later rejected and rebuffed by colleagues and friends. But in his own turn he had a special care for others. He could turn his experience of pain into a capacity for understanding. He made his own heart a home for the homeless. Through spreading his faith in the love of God, millions born after him have dwelt 'in the house he shaped in his heart.'

The priest and Mary

If we want to fathom our role in the mystery of salvation we should fix our gaze on the Mother of Christ, for, as *Redemptor hominis* has it, 'the redemption took place beneath the heart of Mary.' But it happened in her body only because it could happen in her heart: only because it was a virgin heart, a single-minded heart. Augustine was a man of pithy aphorisms and one was *Maria concepit Christum prius mente quam ventre*: she conceived Christ first in her heart and then in her body. Or, as the less succinct phrase of a modern hymn says it:

> O with what joy we sing of Mary
> A woman of great love
> Whose openness and loving kindness
> Gave birth to God's own Son.

She was so generously attuned to God's will that he could be himself *with* her. *In* her. In Mary, preparation for God reached its peak of perfection; acceptance was absolute. In virgin selflessness, in immaculate generosity, she made herself most totally available for the embodiment and expression of God's redemptive love. In that sense, an English poet could rightly declare her 'our tainted nature's solitary boast!'

Not that this can place a gulf between Mary and the rest of us. Mary is not an island set out in the sea, separated from the rest of humanity. She is the furthest tip of the promontory of the mainland of humanity reaching nearest to God. She can only be one of us and always part of our lives.

But she is more than one of ourselves. She is our mother. The first Christmas she carried the first-born but ever since she has been carrying us. She is mother not just of Christ but of all the living — all conceived of the Holy Spirit and born of God. Augustine had a lovely phrase for the mystical body. He called it 'the whole Christ' and said,

> For there is only one man who reaches out till the end
> of time — and all men are this man and this man is
> all men — Christ united with His Church.

As the vocation of the little Nazareth mother unfolded, her initial agreement to bear Christ had to become the deeper basis for an intensified motherhood of the *mystical* Christ. And to me her mystical motherhood must mean that Mary is still somehow in labour and still anxious until the *whole* Christ is formed; until the *whole* Christ is born. In the birth and growth of all her Son's members, Mary is dedicating herself with a mother's sacrifice and a mother's love. Far from obscuring the centrality of her Son's work, she facilitates and fosters it. Seen from her vantage-point — merged with her motherhood — the mystery of Christ's redemption becomes more meaningful.

For example, when she calls us to re-live in ourselves each day the fifteen mysteries of her Son's life from his conception and birth until his cross and resurrection we discover that his mother doesn't disturb but rather distils our union with Jesus.

We discover that she is merely alerting us to *our annunciations*: that our response like hers will be shaped through surrender to the Spirit of God and forged on the anvil of persistent, pondering prayer so as to issue in our free gift of the prince of peace and permanence to a weary world of fragile hopes and broken promises.

We discover why her *visitations* have been continuous and countless down the centuries challenging complacency and causing hearts to convert and leap for joy at the nearness of their Saviour.

We discover above all that in the *Nativity* she restlessly readies the manger of our hearts to receive the wonder of divine life, training us to turn from the traps of triviality; from tinkering with tinsel, and treading over the *real truth* — because in the couplet of the German poet,

Had Christ a thousand times in Bethlehem been born
But not in thee
For all eternity thou art forlorn.

We discover her still at work to complete her *presentation in the temple* of their father's house, all Christ's body.

We discover her searching still because her family is as yet partly lost and will be till the *whole* Christ is found.

We discover that she *sorrows* still — sharing the prolonged agony in the world of her Beloved Son touched by every scourge that now afflicts his members, sharing their diminished dignity and the thorns of their degradation.

We find that she wanders the road of life to meet her grieving children beneath their crosses for her Son is under *every* cross. And she will not leave the hill of crucifixion because he cannot be taken down and placed across her wounded heart as long as one of us still remains impaled by nails of pain. For it is by the cross when the Church was born from his perforated heart that he consigned us to her in his tender statement:

This is *your* mother : this is *your* son.

As Queen of Glory, *risen* in Christ's power and *ascended* as pattern of our perfection Mary's maternity can never be interrupted till all her Son's brothers and sisters have journeyed through their dangers and difficulties and shared his glory which is the fullness of the Holy Spirit for whom she began praying with the infant Church in the upper room.

If she cradled Christ from crib to cross 'with love beyond all telling', it is only in deep prayer that we can hope to appreciate the unspeakable tenderness with which she holds *us* individually. If we understood the delicacy of her motherliness we — especially priests — would surely 'weep with joy'. An incident recorded in Cardinal Heenan's autobiography underscored this for me. In *Not the Whole Truth* he recalled 'the battle for his vocation' and even after fifty years he could remember the painful details. He had recovered from serious illness and was allowed to convalesce with another student's family in the Durham countryside. Needless to say he relished the glorious month of freedom pampered with home cooking and clear of the rigours of the tough seminary and even from the authority of his own home. But in addition he met a charming girl of his own age and when at last he had to return to the seminary, he felt incredibly miserable. Thinking of his girl-friend constantly, the seminary seemed a prison. The separation oppressed him and even prayer seemed to fail him. He couldn't endure the separation. Yet he spoke to no one about his pain. The Mass which had always been a source of strength seemed to fail him. The enthusiasm for a priest's life, built up carefully over the years, seemed deflated. He couldn't go on; he had to decide.

On the next half-day, instead of walking, he spent the afternoon in the deserted college chapel. For hours he wrestled with the problem. Was he strong enough to make the sacrifices required of a candidate for the priesthood? Could he be happy without his beloved? Could he give up the right to be a husband and father? Light on the problem did not come at once but by early evening he was convinced he had no vocation to the priesthood.

Quite calm after reaching his decision, he paid a visit to the shrine of our Lady on the way out. He thanked her that his mind was made up. At once all his doubts flooded back. He looked up at the altar cloth and the words embroidered 'Show yourself a mother' and with a blinding clarity he suddenly saw his problem in simple terms. In fact he had no problem. God was calling him to be one of his priests but he wasn't prepared to give up the comforts of human love to follow him. God was calling him to be a priest but he needed a tender loving person beside him at the same time. That evening he found both! In the throes of discomfort and homesickness he found his mother. And never again in his long life was he troubled with doubts about his vocation. And on that day a relationship with our Lady began which was to be the driving-power of his priesthood, ever after. And these were not fanciful memories penned by a naive sentimentalist in a flurry of emotion or poetic reverie. They were recalled after fifty years of a rich life by a man well-known for his practical ability and outstanding courage; a man well-seasoned by a curate's work with the poor of Barking and as parish priest in London's East End, a philosopher, a man whose executive ability, more than anything, probably recommended him for bishop, a man whose keen wit sparkled before even the sharpest and Frostiest (!) of B.B.C. interviewers.

And yet, throughout his fifty years of outstanding priestly work it was his firm conviction that the nearness of this gracious lady convinced him of his capabilities, calmed his worry, regaled his flagging spirit, and engendered his enthusiasm — as she had done the evening he nearly left the seminary. It was she who, by her gentle power and tender strength, drove him on to give of his best. Maybe there's sense in the old tag, 'Behind every great man there's a great woman!'

A classfriend of my own — now a contented and vigorous priest — once remarked to me in a moment of honest soul-searching, 'What I'm going to miss most of all through not getting married, is having someone close by me, whose nearness would always force me to give of my best; who would believe so much in me as to keep saying, ". . . Ah now, you can do better than that", when I'd finished some piece of work, or "Why don't you try that again . . ." — someone who wouldn't allow me to settle for the mediocre.'

And I listened carefully because I noticed he was discussing celibacy, not in the self-pitying tones we're so used to hearing; he was wondering more about its effect on his daily work and performance than as diminishing his personal happiness. Obviously his insights into good family life showed him that the proper wife is attuned to a husband's deepest needs; she can take his worry in her stride — just as easily as she can take the children's bruised knees or cut fingers! She soothes, she listens, she supports. He has confidence in her because she's a sort of catalyst, setting things going, planning, devising, and encouraging the family to do better, to give of their best; never letting life grind to a halt for them; seeing new possiblities and goading them on, more by her quiet expectations than irksome pressure. And when he had finished speaking it occurred to me that he had been outlining, fairly accurately, how the power of the gentle lady, the Virgin Mary, could heighten and strengthen the performance of the priest in his daily work. It's hardly an accident that when Christ, in his dying breath, broadened her motherhood to include all God's children, the gift was made through a young priest who had dared to keep her company beneath the cross.